THE JEHOVAH'S WITNESSES AND PROPHETIC SPECULATION

THE JEHOVAH'S WITNESSES AND PROPHETIC SPECULATION

An Examination and Refutation of the Witnesses'
Position on the Second Coming of Christ,
Armageddon and the "End of the World"

by

Edmond Charles Gruss

PRESBYTERIAN AND REFORMED PUBLISHING CO.
Box 817, Phillipsburg, New Jersey

Copyright © 1972
Presbyterian and Reformed Publishing Co.
Second edition, December, 1975
Seventh printing, May, 1983

ISBN: 0-87552-306-4

Printed in the United States of America

This book is affectionately dedicated to the memory of my mother Frieda Elise Gruss (1898-1966) who received Christ as her Saviour and declared: "I believe that Jesus Christ died on the cross for my sins."

THE AUTHOR

Edmond C. Gruss, Professor of History and Apologetics at The Master's College, in Newhall, California, was born in Los Angeles in 1933. He received his A.B. from Los Angeles Baptist College (1955) and his B.D. from Los Angeles Baptist Theological Seminary (1958). In 1961 he completed the Th.M. in Bible and Theology at Talbot Theological Seminary, La Mirada, California. An M.A. in Modern European History was added in 1964.

In addition to his college and seminary teaching Professor Gruss has written articles on the cults and given lectures in area churches. In 1970 he authored the book *Apostles of Denial: An Examination and Expose of the History, Doctrines and Claims of the Jehovah's Witnesses.* Interest in the cult field stems from his conversion from the Jehovah's Witnesses in 1950. His wife also graduated from Los Angeles Baptist College and is an elementary school teacher. The family includes two teen-aged children.

Reflecting his interests, the author is a member of The American Historical Association, Organization of American Historians, Far West Slavic Conference, Society for Early Historic Archaeology, Creation Research Society, and The Conference on Faith and History.

ACKNOWLEDGMENTS

My gratitude is expressed to Dr. Richard D. Patterson of Los Angeles Baptist College and Theological Seminary for his comments and advice in the work of revision and rewording in the manuscript of this book. My appreciation is also given to his wife Ann who typed the final draft. I wish to thank Dr. Edwin R. Thiele for his correspondence on Bible chronology, Mr. Richard F. Miller for locating *Three Worlds* and other sources, and Mr. Maurice Barnett for the Scotland trial microfilm. I am also grateful for the assistance of my family, especially my wife Geraldene, who spent hours in typing and proofreading. And finally, I wish to thank Mr. Charles Craig, editor, Presbyterian and Reformed Publishing Company, for his interest in this study and its publication.

TABLE OF CONTENTS

CHAPTER	PAGE
1. INTRODUCTION	13
2. THE WITNESSES' POSITION ON THE SECOND COMING OF CHRIST AND "THE END OF THE WORLD"	16
3. AN EXAMINATION AND REFUTATION OF THE WITNESSES' POSITION ON THE 1914 SECOND COMING OF CHRIST	20

    The Witnesses' 1914 Predictions ... 20
    The "Appointed Times of the Nations" ... 26
    The Beginning of the "Appointed Times of the Nations" ... 27
        Correspondence with the Watchtower Society ... 28
        Establishing the Date for the Fall of Jerusalem ... 38
    The End of the "Appointed Times of the Nations" ... 42
    The Year-Day Theory ... 43
    The "Time of the End" ... 46
    The Sign of "The Last Days" ... 47

4. AN EXAMINATION AND REFUTATION OF THE WITNESSES' POSITION ON THE 1975 CHRONOLOGY 59

    The Witnesses and the 6000-Year Tradition ... 59
    The Witnesses and Biblical Chronology ... 62
        Confidence in a "Correct" Chronology ... 62
        Chronology Based on Supposition and Faith ... 64
        Chronology and the Creation Date ... 66
        Adam's Stay in the Garden ... 69
    The Witnesses and Biblical Genealogies ... 72
        The Problem of Sources ... 72
        The Probability of Abridged Genealogies ... 72
        The "Second Cainan" of Luke 3:36 ... 75
    Additional Problems with the Witnesses' Chronology ... 76
    The Babylonian Captivity ... 77
    From the Dividing of the Kingdom to the Fall of Jerusalem ... 99

The Date of the Genesis Flood	78
Conclusion	79

5. THE WITNESSES' POSITION ON THE "LAST DAYS" AND ARMAGEDDON: AN ILLUSION OF URGENCY 81

1877-1899	82
1900-1919	84
1920-1929	87
1930-1939	88
1940-1949	90
1950-Present	92
Conclusion	94
APPENDIX Is Time Running Out For the Witnesses?	96

6. FALSE ADVERTISING, FALSE PROPHECY AND FALSE CHRISTIANITY 97

7. CONCLUSIONS AND A PERSONAL TESTIMONY 102

APPENDIXES

A. THE GREAT PYRAMID OF EGYPT	110
B. THE FATHERS AND THE WATCHTOWER ON THE 6,000-YEAR TRADITION	114
C. RUSSELL'S CHRONOLOGY AND ITS VERIFICATION	115
D. WHITCOMB AND MORRIS ON ABRIDGED GENEALOGIES	118
E. ARE THE GENESIS DAYS 7,000 YEARS LONG?	128

FOREWORD

The prophetic claims and interpretations of the Jehovah's Witnesses concerning the second coming ("presence") of Christ in 1914, and the recent speculation that Armageddon was due in the mid-seventies *(1975 or before according to Witness publications), have never been fully examined and refuted in detail. The present study was written because the author concluded after investigation that the Witnesses' position does not accord with the truth and cannot stand objective examination.

The writer challenges the reader with the statement found in the popular Witness book, *The Truth that Leads to Eternal Life*, published in 1968:

> We need to examine, not only what we personally believe, but also what is taught by any religious organization with which we may be associated. Are its teachings in full harmony with God's Word, or are they based on the traditions of men? If we are lovers of the truth, there is nothing to fear from such an examination (p. 13).

If the reader is a Jehovah's Witness, or is studying with the Witnesses, will he demonstrate that he is genuinely objective in his search for the truth and is a "lover of the truth" by his careful examination of what he believes, and has been taught, in the light of this study? As the quotation above states: "If we are lovers of the truth, there is nothing to fear from such an examination."

---

*The current (December 1975) teaching is that Armageddon could occur at any time. Specificially, it is delayed only by the time interval between Adam and Eve's creation.

Chapter 1

INTRODUCTION

The latter half of 1914 marked the commencement of World War I to the vast majority of persons living at the time, but to the followers of Charles Taze Russell and to the Witnesses of today that year had far greater significance. "Beyond all doubt, the evidence points to 1914 as the year when the kingdom of God went into operation, and that event is causing things to happen here on earth."[1] "Both in Bible chronology and in the events that were foretold to take place from 1914 onward we find confirmed beyond doubt that 1914 was the beginning of the end for this present system."[2] The "end for this present system" is placed "within a few years at most" by a Witness writer who then warns: "Time is fast running out for it! It is much later for this world than you may think! Indeed, it has only a few more years of existence left."[3] The specific year for the terminal point of the present order was given as 1975.[4] The significance of 1975 was stressed in the following quotation:

> ... Six thousand years from man's creation will end in 1975, and the seventh period of a thousand years of human history will begin in the fall of 1975 C.E..... It would not be by mere chance or accident but would be according to the loving purpose of Jehovah God for the reign of Jesus Christ, the "Lord of the sabbath," to run parallel with the seventh millennium of man's existence.[5]

---

[1] *The Truth that Leads to Eternal Life* (Brooklyn: Watchtower Bible and Tract Society, 1968), p. 93.

[2] *Awake!*, XLIX (October 8, 1968), p. 6.

[3] *Ibid.*, p. 4.

[4] *Ibid.*, p. 14.

[5] *Life Everlasting—in Freedom of the Sons of God* (Brooklyn: Watchtower Bible and Tract Society, 1966), pp. 29, 30. See the Appendix update, pp. 96f.

The crucial importance of 1914. As the quotations above indicate, the Witnesses believe that in 1914 God's heavenly kingdom was established and the "end of this present system" began. It is also explained that at that time a war was fought in heaven and Satan and his evil hosts were cast down to earth.[6] The establishment of the kingdom in heaven and the enthronement of Christ as the king makes it necessary for those faithful to God to proclaim the "good news of the kingdom."[7] Much additional understanding of their doctrine and prophecy relates to the 1914-established kingdom claim, such as: the resurrection of the dead in Christ in 1918, the laying of the foundation of the "new earth"[8] and the fall of Great Babylon in 1919.[9]

The 1914 date has been one of the most emphasized doctrines advanced by the Witnesses. They take the position that the Watchtower Society must be God's visible organization because it alone through its publications first discerned and now stresses this year as specially marked by Jehovah. However, if the Witnesses are wrong concerning this date, not only would the claim that the Society represents God's visible organization and "channel" for the revelation of His truth for this age be invalidated, but the major teachings in a number of Witness books and magazines must, of necessity, be rejected (e.g., *Babylon the Great Has Fallen! God's Kingdom Rules!*—published in 1963; *The Watchtower,* "What Has God's Kingdom Been Doing Since 1914?"—October 15, 1968).

The importance of 1975. In 1966, Witness leadership not only stressed that the year 1975 was the end of 6,000 years of human history, but also speculated that Armageddon could occur the same year. Much speculation as to what would occur characterized the years before 1975 — speculation which was not realized in the events which transpired. It is the contention of this writer that the stress on the 1975 date was just another example of erroneous Watchtower speculation, a manufactured illusion of urgency, to gain converts, to restore the inactive, and

---

[6] *From Paradise Lost to Paradise Regained* (Brooklyn: Watchtower Bible and Tract Society, 1958), pp. 175, 176.

[7] *Ibid.,* p. 177.

[8] *Ibid.,* pp. 192, 214, 215.

[9] *Babylon the Great Has Fallen! God's Kingdom Rules!* (Brooklyn: Watchtower Bible and Tract Society, 1963), pp. 500, 504, 510.

For an extended list of important events and developments connected with 1914 see: *Then Is Finished the Mystery of God* (Brooklyn: Watchtower Bible and Tract Society, 1969), p. 373 f.

to press Witness ministers to greater activity. As with the 1914 failure, and many others, this latest error seriously questions the claim that the Society is God's "channel" and clearly identifies it as a false prophet.

The organization of the study. Beyond this introduction, the study proceeds in the following fashion. Chapter 2 presents a survey of the Witnesses' position on the subjects under discussion. Chapters 3 and 4 are devoted to an examination and refutation of the Witnesses' claims. Chapter 5 demonstrates by a chronological approach that since their beginning the Jehovah's Witnesses have stressed the soon outbreak (or actual beginning) of Armageddon and the "end of the world." It will be seen that in this way they have created an *illusion* of urgency which is not based upon the Bible but upon human speculation. Chapter 6 cites the statements of Witness publications and leaders which reveal that the Society is guilty of false advertising and false prophecy, causing this writer to conclude that this system presents a false Christianity. Chapter 7 reviews some of the conclusions reached and answers the question which relates to the author's experiences: "Why a Witness of Jesus Christ—Not a Jehovah's Witness?" Several Appendixes include material of importance, but not vital to the major developments presented in the body of the book.

It has not been the intention of this writer to examine or explore in depth every area of the Witnesses' eschatology; rather, it is his thesis that if the two key dates, 1914 and 1975 (especially 1914) can be shown to be in error, many other claims relative to their doctrine and prophetic interpretation are therefore without foundation. It is also this author's contention that the Witnesses' own materials demonstrate clearly that they have been untrustworthy interpretors of prophecy.

Chapter 2

THE WITNESSES' POSITION ON THE SECOND COMING OF CHRIST AND THE "END OF THE WORLD"

This chapter presents a summary of the line of argument used in the publications of the Jehovah's Witnesses in the establishment of their prophetic program relative to Christ's second coming and to the "time of the end" and its termination.

The Witnesses predicted the significance of 1914 many years before:

> In the "Watchtower" magazine of March, 1880, they said: "The Times of the Gentiles extend to 1914, and the heavenly kingdom will not have full sway till then." Of all people, only the witnesses pointed to 1914 as the year for God's kingdom to be fully set up in heaven.[1]

How did the Witnesses arrive at that date? In Luke 21:24 it is recorded that "Jerusalem will be trampled on by the nations, until the appointed times of the nations are fulfilled" (NWT).[2] What is the significance of this statement?

> The "appointed times of the nations" indicated a period in which there would be no representative government of Jehovah on earth, such as the kingdom of Israel was; but the Gentile nations would dominate the earth.[3]

When did God's earthly kingdom end and the "appointed times of the nations" begin?

---

[1] *From Paradise Lost to Paradise Regained*, p. 170.

[2] The expressions "times of the Gentiles" and the "appointed times of the nations" are synonymous.

[3] *Let God Be True* (second ed., 1952; Brooklyn: Watchtower Bible and Tract Society, 1946), p. 250.

SECOND COMING AND END OF WORLD

God's earthly nation or kingdom ended when a pagan king destroyed Jerusalem. This pagan king was Nebuchadnezzar, king of Babylon.... The king of Babylon took Zedekiah off "Jehovah's throne" in the year 607 B.C. and laid his city and territory desolate. So that year God's earthly kingdom ended. And that year, 607 B.C., the "appointed times of the nations" began.[4]

When did the "appointed times of the nations" end? The background for the answer is found in Daniel 4, in the prophetic dream of Nebuchadnezzar.

The prophetic dream disclosed a great tree which grew from the earth and reached to heaven and furnished food and shelter to all creatures. Suddenly a holy one from heaven commanded: "Hew down the tree,... nevertheless leave the stump of his roots in the earth, even with a band of iron and brass,... and let seven times pass over him."[5]

What does this dream mean?

"Seven times" meant seven literal years in the case of Nebuchadnezzar, deprived of his throne. The seven years were equal to 84 months, or, Scripturally allowing 30 days for each month, 2,520 days. At Revelation 12:6, 14, there are 1,260 days mentioned and described as a "time, and times, and half a time," or 3 1/2 times. Seven times would be twice 1,260 days, or 2,520 days.[6]

The 2,520 days are to be understood as years. "By his faithful prophet Ezekiel Jehovah said: 'I have appointed thee each day for a year.' (Ezekiel 4:6) By applying this divine rule the 2,520 days mean 2,520 years."[7]

The Witnesses therefore arrived at the following conclusion:

... Since God's typical kingdom with its capital at Jerusalem ceased to exist in the autumn of 607 B.C., then, by counting the appointed times from that date, the 2,520 years extend to the autumn of A.D. 1914.[8]

They found further proof that 1914 "marked the beginning of the 'time of the end' " with the establishment of the kingdom in heaven in the fulfillment of prophecy.[9]

---

[4] *From Paradise Lost to Paradise Regained*, pp. 171, 172.

[5] *Let God Be True*, p. 251.

[6] *Ibid.*, pp. 251, 252.

[7] *Ibid.*, p. 252.

[8] *Ibid.*

[9] *Ibid.*, p. 253 f.

18 THE JEHOVAH'S WITNESSES AND PROPHETIC SPECULATION

> Exactly what did Jesus point to as marking his second presence and the "conclusion of the system of things"? He said: "Nation will rise against nation and kingdom against kingdom, and there will be food shortages and earthquakes in one place after another" (Matt. 24:7).[10]

A number of other indications of being in the "last days" are seen by the Watchtower writers, for example: pestilences (Luke 21:11), increasing lawlessness (Matt. 24:12), the preaching of the "gospel of the kingdom" (Matt. 24:14), men seeking pleasure instead of God (II Tim. 3:4).[11]

To them, all of the foregoing "allow for only one meaning: that we have been in the 'last days' since 1914."[12]

Thus, the 1914 date is established and verified in two ways: by Bible chronology and by the fulfillment of prophecy.

The Witnesses believe that the consummation of "the time of the end" is very near. How is this known? In two ways:

> One way is by noting what Jesus said when he gave his great prophecy about the "last days." After he listed the many events that would mark this period, he also stated: "Truly I say to you that this generation will by no means pass away until all these things occur" (Matt. 24:34).
>
> ... Jesus was saying that some of those persons who were alive at the appearance of the "sign of the last days" would still be alive when God brought this system to its end.[13]
>
> There is another way that helps confirm the fact that we are living in the final few years of this "time of the end." (Dan. 12:9) The Bible shows that we are nearing the end of a full 6,000 years of human history. What significance does this have?
>
> ... Revelation chapter 20, verse 6, shows that God's heavenly kingdom will rule over the earth for one thousand years after the end of this system of things. That millennium will bring a sabbathlike rest to the earth and all those then inhabiting it. Hence, the first six thousand years since man's creation could be likened to the first six days of the week in ancient Israel. The seventh one-thousand-year period could be likened to the seventh day, the sabbath of that week.—2 Peter 3:8.

---

[10] *The Truth That Leads to Eternal Life*, p. 86.

[11] *Awake!*, XLIX (October 8, 1968), pp. 9-12. See these pages for further evidences.

The book *Make Sure of All Things* (Brooklyn: Watchtower Bible and Tract Society, 1953), pp. 337-344, presents some thirty-nine different signs, which to the Witnesses, taken together, comprise the "sign of the last days."

[12] *Awake!*, XLIX (October 8, 1968), p. 13.

[13] *Ibid.*

How fitting it would be for God, following this pattern, to end man's misery after six thousand years of human rule and follow it with His glorious Kingdom rule for a thousand years![14]

In addition, according to "reliable Bible chronology," the full 6,000 years of human existence "will evidently finish in the autumn of the year 1975."[15] Witness vice-president F. W. Franz indicated that the 6,000 years ended at sundown, September 5, 1975, according to the lunar calendar.

---

[14] *Ibid.*, p. 14.

[15] *Ibid.* A detailed presentation of the 6,000-year chronology is found in *All Scripture Is Inspired of God and Beneficial* (Brooklyn: Watchtower Bible and Tract Society, 1963), pp. 283-286.

Chapter 3

AN EXAMINATION AND REFUTATION
OF THE WITNESSES' POSITION
ON THE 1914 SECOND COMING OF CHRIST

It was this writer's contention that the Witnesses' prophetic views could not stand objective examination. This chapter reviews the position of the Witnesses on 1914 as it was presented in the preceding chapter, with some additional details, and then offers a refutation of each point.

I. THE WITNESSES' 1914 PREDICTIONS

The Witnesses contend that they alone successfully predicted that the year 1914 was a pivotal year in Biblical prophecy. In considering this claim it is necessary to again refer to the statement previously cited in Chapter 2:

> In the "Watchtower" magazine of March, 1880, they said: "The Times of the Gentiles extend to 1914, and the heavenly kingdom will not have full sway till then." Of all people, only the witnesses pointed to 1914 as the year for God's kingdom to be fully set up in heaven.[1]

An examination of this citation shows that the comment following the quotation of the March, 1880 *Watch Tower* magazine is an excellent example of how present Watchtower Society authors misrepresent the sources they employ (even their own!). This comment indicates that the Witnesses alone pointed to 1914 "for God's kingdom to be fully *set up in heaven.*" (This

---

[1] *From Paradise Lost to Paradise Regained*, p. 170.

is the Society's *present interpretation* on the kingdom of God.) A careful reading of the March, 1880 *Watch Tower* reveals two significant things: (1) The quotation as cited is not complete, but ellipses are not used. (2) When the entire statement is read in context the kingdom spoken of was to be established *on the earth* (not "set up in heaven") in 1914! The complete quotation reads:

> "The Times of the Gentiles" extend to 1914, and the heavenly kingdom will not have full sway till then, but as a "Stone" the kingdom of God is set up "*in the days* of these (ten gentile) kings," and by consumating them it becomes a universal kingdom—a "great mountain and fills the whole Earth."[2]

To place the charge of misrepresentation beyond all doubt, one might read what Pastor Russell wrote in the third volume of *Studies in the Scriptures* (1891). In this book, he stated that the consummation of the "time of the end" would see "the *full establishment of the Kingdom of God in the earth at A.D. 1914*, the terminus of the Times of the Gentiles" (italics mine).[3] A study of additional materials from the pre-1914 period makes it obvious that the present leadership has chosen to alter the facts.

The predictions for 1914 were a failure! Very few Jehovah's Witnesses have studied the predictions which Russell believed would be realized in 1914 or shortly before. When these are reviewed it is evident that his prognostications totally failed. A rash charge? A Satanic lie? Or, the truth? An examination of the predictions will yield the answer. Because of the importance of this point, the following is reproduced directly from Russell's *The Time Is at Hand*, published in 1889.

---

[2] *Watch Tower Reprints*, I (March, 1880), p. 82.

Just one paragraph above this quotation, the author, J. H. Paton stated: "The parallels of the Two Dispensations seem to indicate that Christ was *due as King,* or in the kingly office in the spring of 1878."

[3] C. T. Russell, *Thy Kingdom Come* (Allegheny, Pa.: Watch Tower Bible and Tract Society, 1891), p. 126.

In this chapter we present the Bible evidence proving that the full end of the times of the Gentiles, *i. e.*, the full end of their lease of dominion, will be reached in A. D.

Times of the Gentiles.

1914; and that that date will be the farthest limit of the rule of imperfect men. And be it observed, that if this is shown to be a fact firmly established by the Scriptures, it will prove:—

Firstly, That at that date the Kingdom of God, for which our Lord taught us to pray, saying, "Thy Kingdom come," will obtain full, universal control, and that it will then be "set up," or firmly established, in the earth, on the ruins of present institutions.

Secondly, It will prove that he whose right it is thus to take the dominion will then be present as earth's new Ruler; and not only so, but it will also prove that he will be present for a considerable period before that date; because the overthrow of these Gentile governments is directly caused by his dashing them to pieces as a potter's vessel (Psa. 2:9; Rev. 2:27), and establishing in their stead his own righteous government.

Thirdly, It will prove that some time before the end of A. D. 1914 the last member of the divinely recognized Church of Christ, the "royal priesthood," "the body of Christ," will be glorified with the Head; because every member is to reign with Christ, being a joint-heir with him of the Kingdom, and it cannot be fully "set up" without every member.

Fourthly, It will prove that from that time forward Jerusalem shall no longer be trodden down of the Gentiles, but shall arise from the dust of divine disfavor, to honor; because the "Times of the Gentiles" will be fulfilled or completed.

Fifthly, It will prove that by that date, or sooner, Israel's blindness will begin to be turned away; because their "blindness in part" was to continue only "*until* the fulness of the Gentiles be come in" (Rom. 11:25), or, in other words, until the full number from among the Gentiles, who are to be members of the body or bride of Christ, would be fully selected.

Sixthly, It will prove that the great "time of trouble such

The Time is at Hand.

as never was since there was a nation," will reach its culmination in a world-wide reign of anarchy; and then men will learn to be still, and to know that Jehovah is God and that he will be exalted in the earth. (Psa. 46:10) The condition of things spoken of in symbolic language as raging waves of the sea, melting earth, falling mountains and burning heavens will then pass away, and the "new heavens and new earth" with their peaceful blessings will begin to be recognized by trouble-tossed humanity. But the Lord's Anointed and his rightful and righteous authority will first be recognized by a company of God's children while passing through the great tribulation—the class represented by *m* and *t* on the Chart of the Ages (see also pages 235 to 239, VOL. I.); afterward, just at its close, by fleshly Israel; and ultimately by mankind in general.

Seventhly, It will prove that *before that date* God's Kingdom, organized in power, will be in the earth and then smite and crush the Gentile image (Dan. 2:34)—and fully consume the power of these kings. Its own power and dominion will be established as fast as by its varied influences and agencies it crushes and scatters the "powers that be"—civil and ecclesiastical—iron and clay.

---

* The Greek word here rendered "times" is *kairos*, which signifies *a fixed time*. It is the same word translated "times" in the following passages: Mark 1:15; 1 Tim. 6:15; Rev. 12:14; Acts 3:19; 17:26. The word "seasons" in Acts 1:7 is from the same Greek word.[4]

---

[4] C. T. Russell, *The Time Is at Hand* (Allegheny, Pa.: Watch Tower Bible and Tract Society, 1899), pp. 76-78. Changes have been made in later editions.

As 1914 came and passed, all Russell could salvage from his predictions was the date—all else had failed. Certainly God's kingdom had not been "established in the earth," nor had the kingdoms of the world been destroyed. There was no evidence that the last member of the church had been glorified. Neither natural Israel nor Jerusalem had been restored to favor. Universal anarchy did not characterize the period.

What was Russell's response? In spite of the 100 percent failure, 1914 was not rejected and in September, 1916, he wrote:

> It still seems clear to us that the prophetic period known as the Times of the Gentiles ended chronologically in October, 1914. The fact that the great day of wrath upon the nations began there marks a good fulfillment of our expectations.
>
> . . . .
>
> We see no reason for doubting, therefore, that the Times of the Gentiles ended in October, 1914; and that a few more years will witness their utter collapse and the full establishment of God's kingdom in the hands of Messiah.[5]

A reading of the article which sets forth the statements above reveals a total absence of Scriptural justification for the claims made. Actually, Russell's chronology had nothing more to offer beyond 1914.

Two additional observations are worthy of notice. (1) The First World War as "a good fulfillment of our expectations," should rather be viewed as an additional failure of Russell's claims for 1914 (a point which is explained below). (2) The "few years" before the consummation also failed.

Did Russell predict World War I? Although Jehovah's Witnesses at present claim that World War I was predicted by Russell,[6] this contention is totally false.

Russell was definite as he wrote:

> In view of this strong Bible evidence concerning the Times of the Gentiles, we consider it an established truth that the final end of the kingdoms of this world, and the full establishment of the Kingdom of

---

[5] *Watch Tower Reprints,* VI (September 1, 1916), p. 5950.

[6] *Jehovah's Witnesses in the Divine Purpose* (Brooklyn: Watchtower Bible and Tract Society, 1959), pp. 54, 55; *The Watchtower,* XC (February 1, 1969), pp. 71, 72.

God, will be accomplished at the end of A.D. 1914 [The 1915 edition reads: "Will be accomplished near the end of A.D. 1915."].[7]

In the light of this statement the coming of the First World War actually showed Russell's chronology to be wrong; for while he predicted the consummation of the age at the end of 1914, the war continued until 1918.

A long-time student of the movement (who had been a Witness for more than thirty-one years) also denied that Russell predicted World War I.

> We challenge all Truth Movement leaders of every vintage to cite for us even ONE paragraph or many, from the Pastor's writings before 1914, in Tower or Volumes, where he predicted a World War in 1914. If he ever did predict a World War in 1914, then he predicted the "Irreparable WRECK" of all his predictions about the King and the Kingdom in 1914.[8]

Alan Rogerson agrees that Russell did not predict the European war in 1914 and sees the interpretation as a later addition.

> The Witnesses today claim that in some way Russell predicted World War I, but as far as Russell was concerned the beginning of a war in far-off Europe was little consolation for heavenly glory. Pastor Russell, and his successor Rutherford, saw no great significance in World War I at the time and it was some years later that Jehovah's Witnesses attributed this "prophecy" to Russell.[9]

Russell admitted the vulnerability of his chronology. Very few Jehovah's Witnesses have ever read Russell's admission that his chronology was vulnerable and would be made an "irreparable wreck" if his predictions were not realized in 1914. The following statement was first published in the *Watch Tower* of October 1, 1907 and then reprinted in the December 15, 1913 issue.

> ... Suppose that A.D. 1915 should pass with the world's affairs all serene and with evidence that the "very elect" had not all been "changed" and without the restoration of natural Israel to favor under

---

[7] *The Time Is at Hand,* p. 99.

[8] *Back to the Bible Way,* XV (November-December, 1966), p. 485. Roy D. Goodrich, editor of the magazine, has rejected a number of the doctrines of the Jehovah's Witnesses, but he is still basically unorthodox in theology.

[9] *Millions Now Living Will Never Die* (London: Constable and Company, Ltd., 1969), p. 30.

the New Covenant (Rom. 11:12, 15). What then? Would not that prove our chronology wrong? Yes, surely! Would not that prove a keen disappointment? Indeed it would! *It would work irreparable wreck* to the parallel dispensations and Israel's double, and to the Jubilee calculations, and to the prophecy of the 2300 days of Daniel, and to the epoch called "Gentile Times," and to the 1,260, 1,290 and 1,335 days . . . none of these would be available longer [italics mine].[10]

It does not make any difference if the present Watchtower leadership has discarded some of the views mentioned above. Russell's conclusion that if these predictions failed, the chronology was wrong, still stands.

What has been seen thus far? The present Witnesses have misrepresented Russell's prediction of a 1914 earthly kingdom. Russell's predictions for 1914 failed completely. Yet, instead of admitting failure, he continued the claim that 1914 was right after all, in spite of his admission that the chronology would be proven wrong by failure of fulfillment. It was also seen that Russell did not predict the coming of the World War. If Russell had proven anything, it was that he was a false prophet (Deut. 18:20-22).

II. THE "APPOINTED TIMES OF THE NATIONS"

Luke 21:24 speaks of Jerusalem being "trampled on by the nations, until the appointed times of the nations be fulfilled" (NWT). The term ("appointed times of the nations")[11] is found only here in the Bible. While accepting the literal fall of Jerusalem and the overthrow of Zedekiah as the beginning of this period, the current Witness interpretation no longer views its conclusion as relating to Jerusalem:

> Since the days of Jesus Christ the earthly city of Jerusalem is not what dounts. Rather, the thing that counts is what the Jewish city of Jerusalem symbolized at the time that it was destroyed. . . . It had symbolized God's kingdom by means of his anointed one of the royal house of David.
>
> . . . .
>
> . . . The end of the Gentile Times in 1914 C.E. was to be marked by

---

[10] *Watch Tower Reprints*, V (October 1, 1907), p. 4067; VI (December 15, 1913), p. 5368.

[11] The expressions "times of the Gentiles" and the "appointed times of the nations" are synonymous.

the revival, the rebirth, of God's kingdom in the hands of his anointed one or Messiah, Christ.[12]

It is clear that contrary to the present view, Russell held to a literal interpretation of the "times of the nations," for he said that from 1914 "forward Jerusalem shall no longer be trodden down of the Gentiles, but shall arise from the dust of divine disfavor, to honor . . . ."[13] Russell's interpretation could not be maintained by the Society because of the failure of the 1914 predictions.

Luke 21:24 is a difficult passage and it has been subjected to many differing explanations. As John F. Walvoord comments: "If all varieties of interpretation be considered, at least half a dozen views could be itemized. In general, however, they can be classified as postmillennial, amillennial and premillennial." [14] Walvoord goes on to explain the diversity of understanding on the subject:

> Hence the expression "the times of the Gentiles" is regarded by some as a period in which Gentiles inherit Israel's blessings, and by others is taken as the season for executing divine judgments upon the Gentiles, especially at the end of the age.
>
> . . . Premillenarians tend to take the expression "trodden down by the Gentiles" in a more literal way as referring to the physical possession of Jerusalem by the Gentiles. Normally, this is not related to inheritance of spiritual blessings, although premillenarians recognize that during the period of the times of the Gentiles there may be special blessings allotted to Gentile believers.[15]

It may be concluded, then, that the Witnesses' interpretation of the term is just one of many, and moreover, stands in opposition to that originally proposed by the founder of the Society, C. T. Russell.

III. THE BEGINNING OF THE "APPOINTED TIMES OF THE NATIONS"

The Witnesses claim that 607 B.C. was the year in which Jerusalem fell and in which Zedekiah the last king on "Jeho-

---

[12] *The Watchtower*, LXXXVII (October 15, 1966), p. 617.

[13] *The Time Is at Hand*, p. 77.

[14] "The Times of the Gentiles," *Bibliotheca Sacra*, CXXV (January, 1968), p. 4.

[15] *Ibid.*, pp. 4, 5.

vah's throne" was overthrown by Nebuchadnezzar. They claim that the "times of the nations" began to count from this date. It is obvious that if these events did not take place in 607 B.C. the Witnesses' chronology cannot be correct, for any future date established on a wrong starting date would always be off the number of years in error.

It is an *established fact,* and it will be proved that the events which the Witnesses date 607 B.C. *did not* and *could not* occur then, but *must* be dated 587/6 B.C.

Correspondence with the Watchtower Society

In an effort to explore the sources available, this writer sent the following letter to the Society:

The reply to the author's letter from the Society is worthy of detailed analysis. To the average reader its contents seem impressive. Does the letter give any real support to the Witnesses' claims? Each paragraph will be examined in succession.

Paragraph 1. In response to the author's request for authorities that would support the Witnesses' chronology the Society writer admits that there is no such support. He makes an understatement when he writes: " ... The chronology as accepted by Jehovah's Witnesses ... does not accord with the chronology commonly accepted by secular authorities. ..." It would have been more accurate to say that their chronology is not in accord with that accepted by *any authorities, religious or secular.* The searcher after truth would ask why there is no support for the Witnesses' position outside of their own movement?

Paragraph 2. Without dealing with all the references in this paragraph, it should be pointed out that Ptolemy's Canon and the references mentioned have been worked into a consistent and harmonious chronology by numerous Bible scholars. That the Witnesses' interpretation of the seventy years of captivity (mentioned in paragraphs 1, 2 and 3) is wrong will be seen in some of the points related later in this development.

It is surprising that anyone who professes to know something about Bible chronology would mention Usher and Hales as relevant. When it is realized that James Usher (or Ussher) lived from 1581-1656, and William Hales' four-volume work, *A New Analysis of Chronology and Geography,* was published in 1830,

Newhall, California
October 11, 1968

Watchtower
117 Adams Street
Brooklyn, New York

Dear Sir:

I read with interest the recent issue of Awake! (Oct. 8, 1968) and the more detailed explanation of chronology in Babylon the Great Has Fallen! God's Kingdom Rules! I was especially interested in the dates assigned to the fall of Jerusalem, the reign of Zedekiah, and the beginning of the reign of Nebuchadnezzar. Also, the statement in the text (p. 138, top) concerning Ptolemy's Canon was noted.

I would appreciate it very much if you would list and give me the names of texts or authorities, either religious or secular, which would support the following dates as set forth in Awake! and the above text.

> Nebuchadnezzar begins his rule as king of Babylon 625 BC
>
> The reign of Zedekiah 617-607 BC
>
> The fall of Jerusalem 607 BC

I would also appreciate documentation that the astronomical canon (Ptolemy's Canon) has been proven false and untrustworthy as it relates to verification by modern astronomers and the rulers of Babylon from 747-539 BC.

Sincerely yours,

Edmond C. Gruss
21143 Placerita Cyn. Rd.
Newhall, California 91321

EG:EI   October 31, 1968

Mr. Edmond C. Gruss
21143 Placerita Canyon Road
Newhall, California 91321

Dear Mr. Gruss:

We are happy to know that you had opportunity to read some of our publications.

On page 138 of the Babylon book, to which you make reference, it was acknowledged that the chronology as accepted by Jehovah's witnesses and as there presented does not accord with the chronology commonly accepted by secular authorities, for Jehovah's witnesses accept the Bible and its statement about the seventy years of desolation, though secular authorities generally discount this. ⟦1⟧

The things to be remembered in this connection are: (1) Ptolemy's Canon places the first year of Nebuchadnezzar in the year 604 B.C.E, (2) That the first year of Nebuchadnezzar was in the fourth year of Jehoiakim, according to Jeremiah 25:1, (3) Jerusalem was destroyed in the nineteenth year of Nebuchadnezzar according to 2 Kings 25:2, 8, (4) Jehoiakim and Zedekiah each reigned eleven years in Jerusalem according to 2 Chronicles 36:5, 11, (5) That the Jews returned to Jerusalem at the end of the seventy years in the first year of Cyrus, 537 B.C.E., which is the generally accepted date in harmony with 2 Chronicles 36:19- 23. Any Bible students who try to harmonize satisfactorily the above chronological records of the Scriptures with the date in Ptolemy's Canon for the first year of Nebuchadnezzar will soon prove to himself the impossibility of the task. The difficulties of the problem are manifest by the fact that, whereas Usher gives the date 588 B.C.E. for the destruction of Jerusalem at the dethronement of Zedekiah, Dr. Hales, an equally celebrated chronologer, places this destruction in the year 586 B.C.E., or two years later than Usher. However, if we accept the united testimony of the sacred writers of the Bible that Jerusalem and the land of Judah lay desolate for seventy years, then the chronological data of the Bible are harmonious. At this chronological period the Holy Scriptures and Ptolemy's Canon cannot be harmonized, not even if it could be supposed that the desolation of seventy years began in the third year of King Jehoiakim as has been assumed by many chronologers to be the meaning of Daniel 1:1-4. It is because of deference to ⟦2⟧

Mr. Edmond C. Gruss
21143 Placerita Canyon Road
Newhall, California 91321

October 31, 1968

Page II

Ptolemy's Canon that Daniel 1:1-4 is supposed by some students to support the idea of the thought that the seventy years began in the third year of Jehoiakim, but this reading of Daniel 1:1-4 directly conflicts with all of the historical accounts of the captivities contained in the book of Kings, Chronicles and Jeremiah, which are comprehensively considered in the book "Babylon the Great Has Fallen!" God's Kingdom Rules!

We cannot admit that the seventy years of desolation of Jerusalem began in the third year of Jehoiakim, for according to the Scriptures the term desolation implies "without an inhabitant," and Jerusalem and the land of Judah were not without inhabitants until after the dethronement of Zedekiah as proved in the Babylon book. We cannot reject the combined prophetic and historical testimonies of Kings, Chronicles and Jeremiah simply on the strength of the aforementioned doubtful misreading of Daniel 1:1, more especially as Daniel 1:1 apparently conflicts with Daniel 2:1. However, the Babylon book shows that there is no real conflict between the two texts.

⟨3⟩

On page 390 you will note in the last paragraph of the footnote an instance of where Ptolemy's Canon is evidently in error, as German Doctor William Hengstenberg shows. He gives as a possible reason for the mistake made by Ptolemy's Canon when assigning to Xerxes a reign of twenty-one years that when Ptolemy complied his list of kings from the record of ancient chronologers he mistook the Greek letters "ia" for ka," which letters respectively stood for the numerals 11 and 21.

⟨4⟩

You might take note of page 655 of volume 5 of the Encyclopedia Britannica, 1959 edition. You would observe that, in regard to Babylonian chronology, the period between 648 B.C.E. and the beginning of the reign of Nabopolassar "is still very obscure; the statement of Ptolemy's Canon cannot exactly accord with the facts." If you personally want to pursue this matter, you can get a copy of Ptolemy's Canon, such as is presented in the Journal of the Royal Asiatic Society for 1861. Then you can compare that with the document known as "Babylonian King List A" and part of the "Babylonian Chronicle" as can be found in Ancient Near Eastern Texts, edited by James B. Pritchard, pages 272 and 301-303. You will see that there are a number of differences between Ptolemy's Canon and this other material.

⟨5⟩

In The Watchtower of November 15, 1968, you will find an article on Egyptian chronology, and in the near future we hope to have an article on Babylonian history and chronology, so you can be reading The Watchtower in the near future and note that material when it is published.

⟨6⟩

Sincerely,

Watchtower B. & S. Society
OF NEW YORK, INC.

it is evident that these men have very little to contribute to the dating of events which are more precisely established by many finds since their time. There has been a steady progress toward the precise fixing of dates since the middle of the nineteenth century.

Paragraph 3. Here the point is made that the seventy years of desolation of Jerusalem could only be accomplished after Jerusalem was without an inhabitant ("the term desolation implies 'without an inhabitant' ") and this did not happen until after Zedekiah was dethroned. (In *Babylon the Great Has Fallen! God's Kingdom Rules!* a number of typical references to prove the point are given; those listed at one point are: Jeremiah 9:11; 4:7; 6:8; 26:9; 32:43; 33:10, 12; Zechariah 7:5, 14.)[16] A study of each reference listed in Jeremiah does not require a period of seventy years of desolation, "without an inhabitant," but rather the ultimate accomplishment of that condition. The Zechariah 7:5, 14 reference speaks of a seventy year period and desolation, but again does not demand a seventy year period of absolute desolation.

That the land of Judah was *not* completely stripped of its population at the fall of Jerusalem, or even after Gedaliah's assassination (II Kings 25:25, 26; Jer. 41:1-3), when many Jews fled into Egypt shortly afterwards, is seen from Jeremiah 52:28-30.

> These are the people whom Nebuchadrezzar took into exile: in the seventh year, three thousand and twenty-three Jews.
>
> In the eighteenth year of Nebuchadrezzar, from Jerusalem there were eight hundred and thirty-two souls.
>
> In the twenty-third year of Nebuchadrezzar, Nebuzaradan the chief of the bodyguard took Jews into exile, seven hundred and forty-five souls.
>
> All the souls were four thousand and six hundred. (NWT)

Reference is here made to three separate deportations, the last *five years after* the fall of Jerusalem. In an attempt to maintain the "without an inhabitant view" another Witness writer explains the Jeremiah 52:30 deportation:

> These, however, were not taken off the land of Judah but were captured when Nebuchadnezzar, as Jehovah's symbolic cup, made na-

---

[16] P. 161.

tions that bordered on the desolated land of Judah drink the bitter potion of being violently conquered.—Jeremiah 25:17-29.[17]

The Jeremiah passage does not justify this understanding. Verse 30 must refer to a deportation from Judah. Why? A reading of Chapter 52 stresses events in Jerusalem and the land of Judah. The three deportations are preceded by the statement: "Thus Judah went into exile from off its soil." (NWT) Verse 28 mentions "Jews," verse 29, "Jerusalem," and verse 30, "Jews." The captives of the three exiles are then totaled as a unit in verse 30. Nations or peoples other than from Judah are foreign to the chapter.

A check of a number of sources which deal with this portion of Old Testament history revealed that without exception, they applied Jeremiah 52:30 to another exile from Judah.[18] Therefore, since there was a deportation *five years after* the fall of Jerusalem, the Witnesses' interpretation which demands seventy years "without an inhabitant," must be rejected.

Paragraphs 4, 5 and 6. Statements here deal with supposed "errors" in Ptolemy's Canon: (1) Ptolemy's Canon is evidently in error as it deals with the reign of Xerxes (following Hengstenberg). (2) The *Britannica* article dealing with chronology mentions that the Canon "cannot exactly accord with the facts" dealing with the period between 648-626 B.C. (3) A check of "Babylonian King List A" and part of the "Babylonian Chronicle" found in Pritchard's *Ancient Near Eastern Texts* shows there are a number of differences between the Canon and this material.

In answer to the foregoing: (1) A check of Hengstenberg's dating (486-474 B.C.) on the reign of Xerxes, that accepted by the Witnesses, does not commend itself to scholars today. For example, Parker and Dubberstein give Xerxes dates as 486-465.[19] (Note that the reference to Xerxes' dates is outside of what this writer's letter asked for—i.e., the rulers of Babylon, 747-539.) Instead of error then, Ptolemy's Canon is again veri-

---

[17] *Ibid.*

[18] See for example: F. F. Bruce, *Israel and the Nations* (Grand Rapids: William B. Eerdmans, 1963), p. 94; William F. Albright, "Babylonian Exile or Captivity," *Americana* (1957), III, p. 636; "Babylonian Captivity," *Encyclopaedia Britannica* (1964), II, pp. 979, 980.

[19] Richard A. Parker and Waldo H. Dubberstein, *Babylonian Chronology 625 B.C.-A.D. 75* (Providence: Brown University Press, 1956), p. 17.

fied. In addition, an error at this point, even if proven, is not at all critical in reference to the 607 B.C. versus the accepted 587/6 B.C. date. (2) Reference to the *Britannica* article is an attempt of the Watchtower writer to make a show of scholarly support. The quotation which deals with Babylonian chronology (648-626 B.C.) and states that "Ptolemy's Canon cannot exactly accord with the facts" does not seriously question the accuracy of the Canon. First, if admitted, an error at this point is not critical concerning the dating of the fall of Jerusalem and related events. Second, the article found in the 1959 edition quoted is definitely out-of-date. When was the article written? In correspondence with the Britannica Library Research Service a reply dated November 15, 1968 was received. It stated in part: "The 1959 treatment is essentially the same as when first written for the 1929 edition; the present article was rewritten in 1963."

Why was the current treatment dealing with Babylonian chronology not used? Let the reader judge from the following quotation:

> Proof of the fundamental correctness of Ptolemy's canon has come from the ancient cuneiform tablets excavated in Mesopotamia, including some that refer to astronomical events, chiefly eclipses of the moon.[20]

(3) This writer did compare Ptolemy's Canon with the sources in *Ancient Near Eastern Texts* and found the Canon in substantial agreement. On the surface there seem to be minor differences, but before a comparison is made it must be understood for what purpose the Canon was compiled. Edwin R. Thiele explains that

> Ptolemy's canon was prepared primarily for astronomical, not historical, purposes. It did not pretend to give a complete list of all the rulers of either Babylon or Persia, nor the exact month or day of the beginning of their reigns, but it was a device which made possible the correct allocation into a broad chronological scheme of certain astronomical data which were then available. Kings whose reigns were less than a year and which did not embrace the New Year's day were not mentioned in the canon.[21]

---

[20] Michael B. Rowton, "Chronology" (Babylonian and Assyrian) *Encyclopaedia Britannica* (1968), V, p. 724.

[21] *The Mysterious Numbers of the Hebrew Kings* (revised ed.; Grand Rapids: William B. Eerdmans, 1965), pp. 216, 217.

Watchtower claims as to the inaccuracy of Ptolemy's Canon remain just that—claims.

Concluding remarks on Ptolemy's Canon. What is the importance of the Canon? Why have the Witnesses consistently been critical of it? Ptolemy's Canon is germaine to the acceptance or rejection of the Witnesses' chronology because it gives a list of kings beginning with Nabonassar of Babylon (747 B.C.) and extending to the Graeco-Roman period. The length of reign of each king listed is given in the Canon. Simply stated, if the work of Ptolemy is correct, the Witnesses are wrong in their 607 B.C. fall of Jerusalem date.

In the *Britannica* article dealing with "Eclipse," and the use of eclipses for chronological purposes, it states:

> The chronology of Ptolemy's canon of kings, which gives the Babylonian series from 747 to 539 B.C., the Persian series from 538 to 324 B.C., the Alexandrian series from 323 to 30 B.C. and the Roman series from 30 B.C. onward, is confirmed throughout by eclipses.[22]

Dr. Edwin R. Thiele, in his masterly work, *The Mysterious Numbers of the Hebrew Kings,* affirms:

> The dates of the Nabonassar era have thus been fully established, and once the method of procedure involved in the reckoning of the years of the kings is understood, the canon of Ptolemy may be used as a historical guide with the fullest confidence.
>
> What makes the canon of such great importance to modern historians is the large amount of astronomical material recorded by Ptolemy in his *Almagest,* making possible checks as to its accuracy at almost every step from beginning to end. Over eighty solar, lunar, and planetary positions, with their dates, are recorded in the *Almagest* which have been verified by modern astronomers....
>
> ...Ptolemy's canon gives precise and absolutely dependable data concerning the chronology of a period beginning with 747 B.C..[23]

Dr. Gleason L. Archer, Jr., author of *A Survey of Old Testament Introduction,* confirms that the Canon has been verified: "Astronomical verification of an eclipse which Ptolemy dated as occurring in 522 B.C. has served as a valued reassurance of his accuracy."[24]

---

[22] J. K. Fotheringham and Bernard Pagel, "Eclipse," (Eclipses in History) *Encyclopaedia Britannica* (1964), VII, p. 910.

[23] Pp. 4, 45.

[24] (Chicago: Moody Press, 1964), p. 279.

O. A. Tofflein's *Ancient Chronology* makes the following reference to Ptolemy's Canon:

> His catalogue, beginning with *Nabonassar* of Babylon and extending to Alexander the Great, gives the length of reign of each king of that period. It has been tested by scholars from every point of view, and has in every case stood the test. It is therefore regarded as one of the most accurate chronological works bequeathed to us by antiquity.[25]

From the statements of the authorities cited it is clear that informed scholars accept the accuracy of the Canon.

It is interesting that in the 1877 publication of *Three Worlds, and the Harvest of this World* by N. H. Barbour and C. T. Russell, Ptolemy's Canon is also recognized as authoritative (at least for the establishment of Cyrus' first year):

> The fact that the first year of Cyrus was B.C. 536 [sic], is based on Ptolemy's canon, supported by the eclipses by which the dates of the Grecian and Persian era have been regulated. And the accuracy of Ptolemy's canon is now accepted by all the scientific and literary world. Hence, from the days of Nebuchadnezzar to the Christian era, there is but one chronology.[26]

Even recent *Watchtower* articles, while rejecting the full implications of the Canon's accuracy, state:

> Even though the length of the reign of the kings of Babylon and Persia, as set forth in Ptolemy's canon, may be *basically* correct, there seems to be no reason for holding that the canon is necessarily accurate in every respect for all periods.[27]

While many scholars have affirmed the accuracy of Ptolemy's Canon, the Witnesses continue to retreat behind vague references to its inaccuracy.

Other articles in the Watchtower. The letter from the Watchtower Society made reference to some articles which would appear in *Watchtower* issues on the subject of chronology. The one dealing with Babylonian chronology was published for February 1, 1969, under the title, "Babylonian Chronology—How Reliable?" Much of the article is a rehash of what has been published elsewhere by the Witnesses. On page 90 of the article the Witness writer began his attack on Ptolemy and in the

---

[25] (Part I) (Chicago: Chicago University Press, 1907), p. 1.

[26] (Rochester: Barbour and Russell, 1877), p. 194.

[27] *The Watchtower*, XC (February 1, 1969), p. 90.

process quoted from Thiele's, *The Mysterious Numbers of the Hebrew Kings*. This writer felt that the treatment on Ptolemy and the quotation would be of interest to Dr. Thiele. A letter was sent along with the article asking for his reaction to the discussion of the Canon and the use of the quotation from his book. His answer, in part, dated January 21, 1971, follows:

> In regard to your request for my comment on the use of my quotation in the WATCHTOWER concerning Ptolemy's Canon, I will say that it is misleading and unscrupulous. It is misleading in that it would give an entirely different impression concerning this important canon of Ptolemy than I hold. It is unscrupulous, because a procedure of this type is not honest.
>
> If the writer of this article had been honest—or informed—he would have known that I use Ptolemy's Canon in an entirely different way than he would have it used.
>
> I have the utmost respect for the Canon, and find myself almost standing in awe of its detailed historical accuracy. The man who wrote it must have had at his finger tips an amazing amount of detail concerning early Near Eastern history, and an astonishing amount of astronomical information fitting in at point after point with specific years of the kings. It is accurate and reliable all along the line. Astronomy is one thing upon which we can depend with complete confidence. And when the eclipses of the Canon are so fully in harmony with the years of the kings, we can be certain that the chronology involved is sound. The Canon is right and Jehovah's Witnesses are wrong.
>
> What would I say about the article in general? I would say that such a writer and reader has no business writing about such a subject. He does not know the facts, or if he does, he does not use them in an honest manner. It reminds me of the way an unscrupulous lawyer would deal with facts in order to support a case he knows not to be sound.
>
> Let us be charitable with the man and say that in his reading he does not read as an informed scholar should. In other words, let us accuse him rather of ignorance than dishonesty.

The letter speaks for itself, and seriously questions the motives and qualifications of the writer of the *Watchtower* article.

The article on Egyptian chronology mentioned in the Watchtower letter was published in the November 15, 1968 *Watchtower*, but it does not apply to the subject at hand. A number of additional articles on chronology and related themes have also appeared in *The Watchtower*.[28]

---

[28] August 15, 1968; December 15, 1968; April 1, 1969; May 15, 1971.

Summary on the Watchtower letter. (1) It was admitted that there are no secular (we add religious) authorities who accepted or supported their position on chronology. (2) Ptolemy's Canon and the Bible have been worked into a harmonious and consistent chronology by Bible scholars, contrary to the Witnesses' claims. (3) The issue was confused with the mention of chronologers such as Usher and Hales who are not relevant to the matter. (4) The "seventy years" of the desolation of Jerusalem need not be years of absolute desolation as the Witnesses claim, for, among other things, a correct understanding of Jeremiah 52:30 proves that there was a deportation five years after the fall of Jerusalem. (5) The supposed untrustworthiness of Ptolemy's Canon was not sustained by the sources the Witness writer cited; in addition, numerous scholars supported the extreme accuracy of the canon for the fixing of Bible and secular chronology. (6) Even Russell and Barbour, as well as the Watchtower writers of the present, have made statements which lend support to the acceptance of the Canon as accurate. (7) Witness articles were examined, especially those dealing with Babylonian Chronology, and these would cause one to question whether the writers were actually equipped or objective enough to deal with the subject. This point is clear from the reaction of E. R. Thiele, who is a *recognized* authority on the subject.

Establishing the Date for the Fall of Jerusalem

Thus far, all that has been written requires the acceptance of the 587/6 date for the fall of Jerusalem, and the rejection of the Witnesses' 607 B.C. date. At this point, the evidence of the "Babylonian Chronicle" is considered. The nature of the evidence and its significance are explained by Jack Finegan:

> A number of cuneiform texts from Babylon in the British Museum, some only recently published, make available portions of a Babylonian chronicle with annals covering much of what was the closing period of the kingdom of Judah. By the correlation of such extra-biblical evidence with biblical data it is possible to state dates in this period with relatively great precision and assurance.[29]

---

[29] *Handbook of Biblical Chronology: Problems of Time Reckoning in the Ancient World and Problems of Chronology* (Princeton: Princeton University Press, 1964), p. 199.

Of particular importance is British Museum tablet 21946 published in *Chronicles of Chaldean Kings* (1956)[30] which establishes the date of the first fall of Jerusalem (with the captivity of Jehoiachin and the accession of Zedekiah) as an *absolute date*.[31] When did this occur according to the information on the tablet? "The date of this conquest of Jerusalem is now known precisely for the first time, namely, the second of Adar (15/16th March 597 B.C.)."[32] With the first fall of Jerusalem established precisely in 597, the terminal point *must* be 587/6, with Zedekiah's defeat after an eleven year reign (II Kings 25:2). The reason for the variable is because

> some uncertainty reigns over the precise mode of reckoning of the Hebrew civil year and of the various regnal years of Zedekiah and Nebuchadrezzar in 2 Kings and Jeremiah. Consequently two different dates are current for the fall of Jerusalem: 587 and 586 B.C. The date 587 is here preferred, with Wiseman and Albright (against Thiele).[33]

A number of articles and books by leading Old Testament and Near Eastern scholars which explain the significance of the newly published portions of the Babylonian chronicles appeared in 1956.[34] These prove beyond a doubt that the Witnesses' 607 B.C. date for the fall of Jerusalem is untenable.

---

30 D. J. Wiseman, (London: Trustees of the British Museum, 1956), pp. 67-74. See also pp. 23-37 for the historical survey and pp. 46-48 for a summary of events.

31 The Watchtower writer in *All Scripture Is Inspired of God and Beneficial*, comments on Bible chronology and defines "absolute dates": "Reliable Bible chronology is based on certain *absolute dates*. An *absolute date* is a calendar date that is proved by secular history to be the actual date of an event recorded in the Bible" (p. 281). By the evidence, and by the foregoing definition, the first fall of Jerusalem (597) the death of Nabopolassar and the accession of Nebuchadnezzar (605) are *absolute dates*.

32 Wiseman, p. 33.

33 K. A. Kitchen and T. C. Mitchell, "Chronology of the Old Testament," *The New Bible Dictionary* (Grand Rapids. William B. Eerdmans, 1962), p. 217.

34 Some selected examples not cited before are:

W. F. Albright, "The Nebuchadnezzar and Neriglissar Chronicles," *Bulletin of the American Schools of Oriental Research* (October, 1956), pp. 28-33.

Noel D. Freedman, "The Babylonian Chronicle," *The Biblical Archaeologist*, XIX (September, 1956), pp. 50-60.

Philip J. Hyatt, "New Light on Nebuchadrezzar and Judean History," *Journal of Biblical Literature*, LXXV (December, 1956), pp. 277-284.

Hayim Tadmore, "Chronology of the Last Kings of Judah," *Journal of Near Eastern Studies*, XV (October, 1956), pp. 226-230.

Edwin R. Thiele, "New Evidence on the Chronology of the Last Kings of Judah," *Bulletin of the American Schools of Oriental Research* (October, 1956), pp. 22-27.

In the article, "The Book of Truthful Historical Dates," in the August 15, 1968 *Watchtower,* the writer marshalls the evidence for the Witnesses' absolute date of 539 B.C. from which all their chronology is calculated. This key date is established in several ways according to the article: (1) by the Nabonidus Chronicle which dates the fall of Babylon (p. 490), (2) by astronomy (p. 490), (3) by recognized authorities, such as Jack Finegan, and Parker and Dubberstein (p. 491), (4) by documentation from history books and the weight of historical scholarship ("so many scholars") (pp. 491, 492), and (5) by the Bible. Although it is not mentioned in this article, *The Watchtower* of May 15, 1971, states that 539 B.C. is also proven by Ptolemy's Canon (p. 316).

The present writer can just as legitimately establish 605 B.C. as an absolute date and from this point determine the fall of Jerusalem was 587/6 B.C. That 605 B.C. is an absolute date is based on exactly the same type of evidence that the Witnesses cite. (1) The Babylonian Chronicle (BM 21946) records the death of Nabopolassar, the accession of Nebuchadnezzar and the Battle of Carchemish as occurring in 605 B.C. (2) The *same* astrological tables quoted by Witnesses to establish the fall of Babylon in 539 (October 12) and the date of Cyrus' decree to permit the Jews to return to Jerusalem and to offer up sacrifices there (October 1, 537), designated "the best astronomical tables available" (p. 493), date the accession of Nebuchadnezzar on September 7, 605 (by dating BM 21946).[35] (3) Recognized authorities accept 605 B.C. as the accession date for Nebuchadnezzar, in fact, the *very authorities* appealed to in *The Watchtower* article! (4) The weight of historical scholarship is universally behind the 605 date. In a letter to Dr. Thiele it was asked:

> How strong is the evidence for the 605 B.C. date for the death of Nabopolassar and the accession of Nebuchadnezzar, as compared with the evidence for the end of Nabunaid's reign and the fall of Babylon?

In his reply dated March 4, 1971, in reference to the 605 date and events, Thiele wrote: "I know of no ancient date with any stronger evidence." He then gave the reasons for his statement.

> First there is the eclipse of 621 in the fifth year of Nabopolassar. Nabopolassar reigned 21 years which would make 605 the year of his

---

[35] Parker and Dubberstein, p. 12.

death and the accession of Nebuchadnezzar. For contemporary evidence on that year see D. J. Wiseman, *Chronicles of Chaldean Kings*, p. 69.

Second, there is the calculated eclipse of 568 in the 37th year of Nebuchadnezzar. Working backwards, that would again take you to 605 as the year of Nebuchadnezzar's accession. Both of these eclipses are listed in my *Mysterious Numbers of the Hebrew Kings*, p. 218.

Now having the year 605 for the beginning of Nebuchadnezzar firmly established, all you need is to go forward from there for the rest of the Babylonian kings. The evidence for these you have in Parker and Dubberstein . . . *Babylonian Chronology*, with which you are acquainted.

You have nothing to fear in 605. Working backwards from there you have the eclipse of 621, and working forwards from there you have the eclipse of 568. How easy ancient chronology would be if we could only do that in a few other places!

(5) The 605 date reconciles perfectly with the Bible. (6) Ptolemy's Canon which establishes the 539 B.C. date the Witnesses need for their chronology, also verifies the 605 date.

With Nebuchadnezzar's accession in 605 B.C., the siege and fall of Jerusalem can be calculated on the basis of what year in Nebuchadnezzar's reign these things took place. The following quotation presents the details:

> The last event in the checkered history of the Southern Kingdom was the siege and destruction of Jerusalem by Nebuchadnezzar. This siege began on the tenth day of the month of Zedekiah's ninth year (II Kings 25:1; Jer. 39:1; 52:4. Cf. Ezek. 24:1, 2), January 15, 588 [Parker and Dubberstein, p. 26. "All Julian dates given hereafter are based on the tables of Parker and Dubberstein."] The next year, in the midst of the siege, Jeremiah was imprisoned, this being the tenth year of Zedekiah and synchronizing with the eighteenth year of Nebuchadnezzar (Jer. 32:1), 587. Famine prevailed, the city was broken, and the king fled the following year—on the ninth day of the fourth month of Zedekiah's eleventh year (II Kings 25:2, 3; Jer. 39:2; 52:5-7), July 18, 586. On the seventh day of the fifth month the final destruction of the city began (II Kings 25:8-10), August 14, 586. This was the nineteenth year of Nebuchadnezzar (II Kings 25:8; Jer. 52:12), which was from Nisan, 586 to Nisan 585, Babylonian reckoning, or Tishri, 587, to Tishri, 586, Judean years.[36]

If one takes the *evidence* which is abundantly available, it is inescapable that Jerusalem fell in 587/6.

---
[36] Thiele, *The Mysterious Numbers of the Hebrew Kings*, pp. 168, 169.

Summary. The Witnesses require a 607 B.C. date for the fall of Jerusalem for their 1914 chronology to be substantiated. It has been established in this section that the historical date must be 587/6 B.C. Scholars agree on this date and archaeological evidence places it beyond debate. Claims and objections made by the Society in correspondence and in their publications cannot stand investigation and often reveal a real bias or ignorance. The identical materials and types of evidence which establish the crucial date of 539 B.C. for the Witnesses also establish the 605 B.C. date, rendering the Witnesses' 607 B.C. date for the fall of Jerusalem impossible. On this point alone, the 1914 date for the end of "the times of the Gentiles" is relegated to the scrap heap of exploded theories.

IV. THE END OF THE "APPOINTED TIMES OF THE NATIONS"

Daniel 4:4-27 gives the account of Nebuchadnezzar's dream and Daniel's interpretation. According to the Witnesses, Nebuchadnezzar's period of madness (vv. 25, 33) symbolized the Gentile nations who would have dominion during the "appointed times of the nations." The Witnesses claim that the "seven times" (vv. 16, 23, 25, 32) were literal in Nebuchadnezzar's case and that by comparison with Revelation 12:6, 14 the "seven times" of Daniel are to be understood as 2,520 days.[37] These are next converted into years which run out in 1914.

In answer, this writer would deny that there is any good reason for acceptance of such an interpretation. But beyond this, there are some pertinent questions and observations which should be stated. (1) Where in the Bible does one find that Nebuchadnezzar's dream has any connection with the "times of the nations"? (2) How can Nebuchadnezzar, during his seven years of madness, *when he was not ruling,* picture Gentile domination or rule? Daniel's interpretation of the dream is clear on this point:

> And you will be driving away from mankind, and with the beasts of the field your dwelling is to become, and the vegetation is what they will give even to you to eat just like bulls; and with the dew of the heavens you yourself will be getting wet .... (v. 25, NWT)

---

[37] A complete treatment of the Nebuchadnezzar type is set forth in *Babylon the Great Has Fallen! God's Kingdom Rules!*, pp. 174-181.

The fulfillment which began twelve months later is given in verse 33:

> At that moment the word itself was fulfilled upon Nebuchadnezzar, and from mankind he was being driven away, and grass he began to eat just like bulls, and with the dew of the heavens his own body got to be wet, until his very hair grew big just like eagles' [feathers] and his nails like birds' [claws]. (NWT)

The emphasis of this passage again separates Nebuchadnezzar from his ruling function. (3) There is no need to find any significance beyond the fulfillment of the dream in the life of Nebuchadnezzar. The dream, its interpretation, its fulfillment and the restoration sequence are all that are required for an understanding of the chapter. Thus, any attempt to give a prophetic meaning to this portion of Scripture is nothing more than an assumption.[38] (4) There is no objective evidence that the "times of the nations" have been terminated. (5) The entire interpretation of the "tree vision" and the "seven times" being 2,520 years, is invalid, since a 1914 terminus for the "times of the nations" has been shown to be wrong. Thus, any method used to arrive at such a date does not demonstrate its validity.

V. THE YEAR-DAY THEORY

In the Witnesses' interpretation, the 2,520 days (based on Daniel's "seven times" and Revelation's 3 1/2 times or "time, and times and half a time") were converted into years and the extent of the "times of the nations" was calculated (607 B.C. +

---

[38] The treatment in the Witnesses own *All Scripture Is Inspired of God and Beneficial* (pp. 140, 142) illustrates the point that the "tree vision" requires no additional fulfillment and is included for our instruction. That Daniel 4 is of prophetic significance and Nebuchadnezzar's "seven times" prefigures the duration of years (2,520) of the "times of the nations" is found in several writers of the nineteenth century and was not unique when Russell accepted the theory. While there may be some, this writer did not find any among twentieth century writers who either held or mentioned the interpretation. In addition, those who held the view terminated the "times of the nations" by the visible, personal return of Christ.

Writers in support of the position include: H. Grattan Guinness, *The Approaching End of the Age* (new ed., revised by E. H. Horne; London: Morgan and Scott, Ltd., 1919), pp. 246, 247. (First published 1878.) R. C. Shimeall, *The Second Coming of Christ* (New York: Henry Goodspeed and Company, Publishers, 1873), pp. 170, 171. E. B. Elliott, *Horae Apocalypticae* (fourth ed.; London: Seeleys, 1851), III, pp. 247, 248.

2,520 years = A.D. 1914). The mathematics are simple, but is the year-day theory valid?

The year-day principle was not known to the early Church. What then is its history?

> It was not until medieval times that Jewish and Christian teachers actually advanced year-dayism .... It was first set forth by the former group in the ninth century, and by the latter three centuries later. Joachim of Floris, in Italy, at the close of the twelfth century, applied it to the 1260 days of Rev. 12.... The writers who immediately followed him were defenders of extreme authority for the Pope.
>
> These historical facts are very damaging to this system of interpretation. Sober men are not likely to favor a principle that "was altogether unknown by the Jewish Church before the Christian era, by the Apostles of our Lord, by the primitive Church, by the Fathers—in short, that no one ever thought of ... during ... the first twelve centuries of Christianity" (S. R. Maitland in *Second Enquirey respecting the prophetic period of Daniel and St. John*, p. 77). Moreover, such men will not have their reservations removed by observing that it originated in apostate Judaism and was developed by the Church of Rome. These considerations give strong reasons for suspecting the validity of the theory.
>
> It is true that most, though not all, of the Reformers, from Wycliffe down, applied the year-day principle to the interpretation of prophecy, but it is plain that they derived it from Rome.[39]

After a two-year study of the Bible, in 1818 William Miller (1782-1849), a New England Baptist farmer, applied the year-day principle and established a date for the return of Christ and the end of the world. This would take place "sometime between Mar. 21, 1843 and Mar. 21, 1844; he finally fixed the date at Apr. 17 or 18, 1844."[40] When the latter date failed, an associate of Miller, Samuel S. Snow set the date of October 22, 1844.[41] From the Millerite movement came the Seventh-day Adventists, who still follow the year-day theory as a keystone for prophetic interpretation.[42]

---

[39] Norman F. Douty, *Another Look at Seventh-day Adventism* (Grand Rapids: Baker Book House, 1962), p. 95.

[40] *Ibid.*, pp. 104, 105.

[41] *Ibid.*, p. 105.

[42] LeRoy Edwin Froom, *The Prophetic Faith of Our Fathers* (Washington, D.C.: Review and Herald, 1954), IV, pp. 871, 872.

It was from the Second Adventists who had predicted that the world would end in 1873 that Russell adopted the year-day principle[43] and it is still followed as essential to prophetic understanding.

The theory was decisively refuted by Samuel P. Tregelles in his book *Remarks on the Prophetic Visions in the Book of Daniel,* first published in 1852.[44]

The year-day theory must establish its validity on a Scriptural foundation to be true. Several lines of argument may be urged against the view to demonstrate that it does not pass the test.

1. Numbers 14:34 and Ezekiel 4:6 are interpreted to mean that "with God each day counts for a year."[45] Numbers 14:33, 34 simply states that because of sin Israel was to suffer "by the number of the days that YOU spied out the land, forty days, a day for a year, a day for a year, YOU will answer for YOUR errors forty years. . . ." (NWT) On this passage, Milton S. Terry concludes:

> Here then is certainly no ground on which to base the universal proposition that, in prophetic designations of time, a day means a year. The passage is exceptional and explicit, and the words are used in a strictly literal sense; the days evidently mean days, and the years mean years.[46]

The same is true of Ezekiel 4:5, 6:

> The days of his prostration were literal days, and they were typical of years, as is explicitly stated. But to derive from this symbolico-typical action of Ezekiel a hermeneutical principle or law of universal application, namely, that days in prophecy mean years, would be a most unwarrantable procedure.[47]

---

[43] *Watch Tower Reprints,* IV, July 15, 1906, pp. 3821, 3822. Some of the Second Adventists were Jonas Wendell, N. H. Barbour, and J. H. Paton.

[44] (Sixth ed.; London: Samuel Bagster and Sons, 1883), pp. 112-127. The section is titled "Note on the 'Year-Day System.' "

A short article by Roy L. Aldrich, "Can the End of the Age be Computed by the Year-Day Theory?" appeared in the April 15, 1958 issue of *Bibliotheca Sacra,* pp. 159-165. Aldrich concludes his article with the statement: "It is time that the year-day theory was recognized for what it is—a principle of error, the use of which contradicts the clear teaching of Christ that the time of His coming is secret" (p. 165).

[45] *From Paradise Lost to Paradise Regained,* p. 173.

[46] *Biblical Hermeneutics* (second ed.; Grand Rapids: Zondervan Publishing House, [n. d.]), p. 387.

[47] *Ibid.*

2. If the two passages mentioned did in fact represent a universal law of prophetic interpretation, it is only reasonable that this law could be easily verified by fulfilled prophecy. Terry cites a number of examples in Scripture which overwhelmingly are against the year-day view. Genesis 7:4 records God telling Noah that "in just seven days more I am making it rain upon the earth forty days and forty nights...." (NWT) Would it be proper to understand these days as years? In Genesis 15:13 God told Abraham that his seed was to be resident in a foreign land and would be afflicted for four hundred years. Are these years to be multiplied by 360 to get the proper understanding? The same point can be made on the sixty-five years of Isaiah; the three years of Isaiah 16:14, and the seventy years of Jeremiah 25:12 (cf. Dan. 9:2). Should Jonah's prophecy which announced the judgment of Nineveh be interpreted as symbolizing forty years? The year-day theory cannot be supported by the only possible understanding of other prophecies, that which Terry calls, "the analogy of prophetic scriptures."[48]

3. One of the strongest arguments against the year-day theory is that all who have utilized the theory and predicted the coming of Christ, the end of the world, or other events have failed in their predictions—in Russell's case a 100 percent failure. Terry expands the point:

> We have lived to see his [William Miller's] theories thoroughly exploded, and yet there have not been wanting others who have adopted his hermeneutical principles, and named A.D. 1866 and A.D. 1870 [and it can be added 1873, 74, and 1914] as "the time of the end." A theory which is so destitute of scriptural analogy and support ... and presumes to rest on such a slender showing of divine authority, is on those grounds alone to be suspected; but when it has again and again proved to be false and misleading in its application, we may safely reject it, as furnishing no valid principle or rule in a true science of hermeneutics.[49]

VI. THE "TIME OF THE END"

It is obvious that the year 1914 cannot be sustained as the end of the "appointed times of the nations," and therefore it

---

[48] *Ibid.*, pp. 387, 388.
[49] *Ibid.*, pp. 389, 390.

also cannot mark the definite beginning of the "time of the end." A study of Watchtower interpretation on this subject reveals a change in understanding.

In reference to the period, C. T. Russell stated: "The 'Time of the End,' a period of one hundred and fifteen (115) years, from A.D. 1799 to 1914, is particularly marked in the Scriptures."[50] (Figure 1) J. F. Rutherford, Russell's successor to the presidency and to doctrinal leadership, published his view in 1921 that the evidence was "sufficient to convince any reasonable mind that we have been in the 'time of the end' since 1799."[51] Rutherford later abandoned this date as having any prophetic significance.[52] The present understanding is that "the 'time of the end' began in 1914; it ends when the Devil's world is destroyed at the 'accomplished end.' "[53] (Figure 2)

The foregoing quotations illustrate how flexible God's claimed direction of the Society has been. The 1799-1914 original setting of the "time of the end" reminds the reader that for Russell 1914 was terminal. The period was also identified as "particularly marked in the Scriptures," and evidence was "sufficient to convince any reasonable mind." Yet, in spite of those recommendations, the period was dropped in favor of the new period, currently 1914-1975-(?).

VII. THE SIGN OF "THE LAST DAYS"

The second area of proof that 1914 marks the beginning of the "last days" is found by the Witnesses in the fulfillment of prophecy since that year. This writer has demonstrated in previous sections that the 1914 date could not find support in Bible chronology—so it naturally follows that the signs could not prove what chronology failed to demonstrate. But the signs will be examined anyway to make the refutation of the Witnesses' position complete.

The Witnesses claim that there are thirty-nine signs which mark the second presence of Christ since 1914 and which are a

---

[50] *Thy Kingdom Come*, p. 23.

[51] *The Harp of God* (revised ed.; Brooklyn: Watch Tower Bible and Tract Society, 1921), p. 239.

[52] *Watch Tower Publications Index 1930-1960* (Brooklyn: Watchtower Bible and Tract Society, 1961), pp. 77, 78.

[53] *From Paradise Lost to Paradise Regained*, p. 178.

sign of "the last days" which will end in this generation. It is explained that:

> Occurance of one or even several happenings together is not sufficient to constitute evidence; all must occur concurrently upon one generation in the foretold series or sequences to make up the one composite sign. At least 39 happenings comprise the sign.[54]

The following are given by the Witnesses as comprising the sign of the "last days."

1. Many False Christian Religions 2. World Wars 3. Widespread Famines 4. Unusual Number of Earthquakes 5. Persecution of Christians 6. Christians Betrayed by Relatives and Friends 7. Christians Hated World-wide over Kingdom Issue and for Upholding Christ's Exalted Office 8. Organized Opposition to Kingdom Work by World Leaders 9. Increased Lawlessness 10. Many Forsaking Christianity 11. Worldwide Preaching of the Established Kingdom as Good News 12. Formation of the League of Nations and the United Nations to Stand in Place of Established Kingdom of God 13. Earth-wide Tribulation on Satan's Organization 14. Lying Signs and Great Wonders Performed in God's Name 15. Presence of Christ and Impending Doom of Satan Discernible Universally 16. "Sun" of Man's Prosperity Darkened by Economic Distress 17. "Moon" of Enlightened Man-Rule becomes Dictatorial, Oppressive Rule of Men 18. Wisdom of World's Starlike Wise Ones Perishes 19. Nations Confused and Perplexed as to Course 20. Men becoming Faint Out of World-wide Fear 21. Restoration of True Worshippers 22. Rapid Culmination of All Events on the One Evil Generation 23. People Overly Concerned with Everyday Affairs of Life 24. God's Choosing of Christians Not Dependent on Family or Friendship Ties 25. Indifferent, Sleepy Condition of World but Wakeful, Studious Attitude of Christians 26. One Organization Selected by God as His Faithful Representative 27. Unfaithful Ones Exposed, Separated and Punished as a Class 28. Separating the People of the Nations into "Sheep" and "Goats" 29. World-wide Expansion of Clean Worship 30. Sore Pestilences and Diseases 31. Moral Degeneracy in Public and Private Life 32. Widespread Juvenile Delinquency 33. Instability and Insecurity World-wide Despite Claims of Leaders 34. Men Seek Relief in Make-shift Organizations, Clubs, Institutions 35. Organized Clergy of Christendom and Evil Slave Manifested in Open Diso-

---

[54] *Make Sure of All Things* (Brooklyn: Watchtower Bible and Tract Society, 1953), p. 337.

bedience 36. Improper Restrictions Placed on Marriage and Eating of Food 37. Work of Jehovah's Witnesses Stopped in 1918 38. Many will Ridicule Sign Though Evidence Conclusive 39. World Powers Say "Peace and Safety" as Final Event.[55]

After a review of a number of the signs, a former Witness, William C. Stevenson, commented:

> Having reviewed some of the evidence brought forward by the Witnesses which confirms them in their belief that this is "the time of the end," the reader may register surprise that such flimsy tenuous evidence could convince an intelligent person.[56]

Upon examination, it is possible to categorize the "signs" into two broad categories: those which relate to the Witness movement since 1914, and those which relate to the conditions in the world which are viewed as peculiarly characteristic of this generation. The latter category is usually featured in the literature for public consumption. It would include such signs as: world wars, famines, pestilences, earthquakes and increasing lawlessness. Many of these signs are found in Jesus' words as recorded in Matthew 24 and Luke 21.

In the illustration from the October 8, 1968 *Awake!* (Figure 3) several key features of the "last days" are given. Notice the first four: "World Wars," "Pestilences," "Earthquakes," "Food Shortages"—all are familiar to the reader. Jehovah's Witnesses accept these as sure indicators of the "last days." Yet, it is interesting to find that C. T. Russell, the founder of the movement and advocator of the 1914 chronology, *did not view these very happenings* as signs of the "last days"! Also, articles were published in the *Watch Tower* by other writers who just as strongly took the same position.

As an example of the first point, a *Watch Tower* reader's question and Russell's answer are cited:

> Does Matt. 24:6 teach that "Wars and rumors of wars" are a sign of the end of the Gospel Age?

---

[55] *Ibid.*, pp. 337-344. The signs above are listed as found, but the Scripture citations have been omitted.

[56] *The Inside Story of Jehovah's Witnesses* (New York: Hart Publishing Company, Inc., 1967), p. 79.

STUDY II.

"THE TIME OF THE END,"
OR "DAY OF HIS PREPARATION."
— DANIEL XI.—

THE TIME OF THE END.—ITS COMMENCEMENT, A. D. 1799.—ITS CLOSE, A. D. 1914.—WHAT IS TO BE PREPARED, AND THE OBJECT.—THE WORLD'S HISTORY PROPHETICALLY TRACED THROUGH ITS CHIEF RULERS.—FROM B. C. 405 TO THIS DAY OF PREPARATION.—THE BEGINNING OF THE TIME OF THE END DEFINITELY MARKED, YET WITHOUT NAMES OR DATES.

THE "Time of the End," a period of one hundred and fifteen (115) years, from A. D. 1799 to A. D. 1914, is particularly marked in the Scriptures. "The Day of His Preparation" is another name given to the same period, because in it a general increase of knowledge, resulting in discoveries, inventions, etc., paves the way to the coming Millennium of favor, making ready the mechanical devices which will economize labor, and provide the world in general with time and conveniences, which under Christ's reign of righteousness will be a blessing to all and aid in filling the earth with the knowledge of the Lord. And it is a day or period of preparation in another sense also; for by the increase of knowledge among the masses, giving to all a taste of liberty and luxury, before Christ's rule is established to rightly regulate the world, these blessings will gradually become agencies of class-power and will result in the uprising of the masses and the overthrow of corporative Trusts, etc., with which will fall also all the present dominions of earth, civil and ecclesiastical. And thus the pres-

Figure 1. The "Time of the End" seen as a period from 1799-1914*

---

* *Thy Kingdom Come*, p. 23

WHY A "TIME OF THE END"

⁴ Although the Kingdom came to power in 1914, Jehovah did not immediately destroy those who were not serving him. How glad we can be of that! For God's long-suffering has afforded us the

4. (a) Why can we be glad that God did not immediately destroy those who were not serving him when his kingdom came to power in 1914? (b) How does the Bible, at 2 Peter 3:9, help us to view this matter properly?

Figure 2. The "Time of the End" seen as *beginning* in 1914†

Figure 3. Some important signs of the "last days"‡

---

† *The Truth that Leads to Eternal Life*, p. 95

‡ *Awake!*, XLIX (October 8, 1968), p. 8

A. No; we think not. Wars and rumors of wars have characterized earth's history, with varying frequency and cruelty, ever since the fall of man. But the Scriptures assure us that the time of the end of the Gospel Age, or end of the dominion of the "prince of this world," will witness a more general and widespread warfare than was ever known before, involving all the powers of earth.

. . . .

So also famines and pestilences and earthquakes are not to be regarded specially as signs of the end. Though they will doubtless be frequent, and perhaps more so in the time of the end, like wars have been a part of Satan's policy from the first.[57]

Note again what Russell *denied* as signs of the "time of the end": "wars and rumors of wars," "famines and pestilences and earthquakes"! But the reader may observe, Russell did emphasize warfare "involving all the powers of earth" and an acceleration of the other factors. This is correct, but as the *ending* features of the Gospel Age in 1914—*not the beginning* of "the time of the end"! The following quotation from a sermon Russell preached during the war further proves the point:

The *present great war* in Europe is the *beginning of the Armageddon* of the Scriptures (Rev. 16:16-20). It will eventuate in the complete overthrow of all the systems of error which have so long oppressed the people of God and deluded the world . . . . We believe the present war cannot last much longer until revolution shall break out [italics mine].[58]

An example of an article in the *Watch Tower* which reflects a rejection of some of the key signs of the "time of the end" currently accepted by the Jehovah's Witnesses, is that by H. Grattan Guinness. It appeared in the September, 1884 issue:

Now consider the subject of the signs of the times. Remarks on this subject are too often made which betray a want of intelligent comprehension of the nature of the signs that are according to Scripture to indicate the "time of the end." A careless reading of our Lord's

---

[57] *Watch Tower Reprints*, I, (March, 1884), p. 605. Compare with C. T. Russell, *The Battle of Armageddon* (Brooklyn: Watch Tower Bible and Tract Society, 1897), pp. 563f.

[58] *Pastor Russell's Sermons* (Brooklyn: People's Pulpit Association, 1917), p. 676.

prophetic discourse on the Mount of Olives seems to be the cause of much of this misapprehension. His predictions of wars and rumors of wars, famines, pestilences, and earthquakes, are quoted as if they and such like things were to be the signs of the end of the age. A little accurate attention to the order of his statements would at once show that, so far from this being the case, he mentions these as the characteristic and common events of the entire interval prior to his coming. Wars and calamities, persecution and apostasy, martyrdom, treachery, abounding iniquity, Gospel preaching, the fall of Jerusalem, the great tribulation of Israel, which has, as we know, extended over 1,800 years; all these things were to fill the interval, not to be signs of the immediate proximity of the second advent. How could things of common, constant occurrence be in themselves signs of any uncommon and unique crisis? What commoner all through the ages than wars and rumors of wars, famines, pestilences, and earthquakes? These, as marking the course of the age, can never indicate its close.

. . . .

... No, there was nothing special to alarm the antediluvians before the day that Noah entered into the ark; nothing special to startle the men of Sodom ere the fire from heaven fell; and like as it was in those days, so will it be in these. All going on just as usual, no single sign to attract the world's attention. "None of the wicked shall understand" the true state of affairs, only the "wise" enlightened by the word of prophecy.[59]

The reader is reminded that this article appeared in *Zion's Watch Tower* and obviously was approved. Acceptance of the position set forth would eliminate most of the thirty-nine signs listed by the present Witnesses as indicators of the "time of the end" beginning in 1914.

In preparation for the treatment at this point, a study was made to determine how the thirty-nine sign happenings of the present Witness position were viewed by Russell and other Society writers in publications before 1914. In *every case*, it was found that the same or parallel passages and the features of the age used by the present Witness writers to prove that the "time of the end" began in 1914, were explained by Russell and others in the Society to characterize: (1) the entire Gospel Age, (2) the "time of the end" as viewed at that time—1799-1914, or (3) the Harvest period, 1874-1914.

---

[59] *Watch Tower Reprints,* I (September, 1884), p. 661.

If presently accepted signs of the "last days" are capable of such flexible interpretation and application, certainly they cannot be used to *prove* that Christ has been invisibly present *since* 1914 and that the "time of the end" began at that time!

Of the many signs stated by the Witnesses in support of their views that the "time of the end" began in 1914, the following were selected as examples of why these and other such signs, cannot be used in support of that date.

1. *Earthquakes.* The *Awake!*, October 8, 1968 issue, quotes *Changing Times:* "In this century earthquakes have killed more than 900,000 people."[60] The May 1, 1970 *Watchtower* cites the same figure and the significance of earthquakes:

> It has been reported that the severity and deadliness of earthquakes have increased markedly since the "time of the end" commenced for this old system in 1914. In fact, over 900,000 persons have died from earthquakes in this century, including close to 1,250 in the United States.[61]

Such statements and statistics appear convincing to the unquestioning reader; but that such actually refute the Witnesses' claims concerning 1914 is not difficult to establish.

In the article on "Disasters" in *Collier's Encyclopedia,* there is a selection of some of the world's major disasters, including earthquakes. In this article, it is found that just two earthquakes which occurred early in the twentieth century, *before 1914,* caused the deaths of 520,000. This is *more than half* of the 900,000 which were used as "evidence" that the "time of the end" *began* in 1914!

> *1905.* April 4. Four villages were razed and 370,000 persons killed in an earthquake felt over an area of 1,000,000 square miles in central India. . . .
>
> *1908.* December 28. The great Messina earthquake killed 150,000 persons in southern Italy and Sicily, including 85,000 in the city of Messina alone, which was totally destroyed. This was one of the most disasterous of recorded earthquakes.[62]

---

[60] XLIX, p. 9.

[61] XCI, p. 270.

[62] Eileen Teclaff, (1964), VIII, p. 254.

It may interest the reader that earthquakes have been studied instrumentally only since early in the twentieth century, and "if all earthquakes down to zero magnitude could be detected, the number would be between one and ten million each year." John H. Hodgson, *Earthquakes and Earth Structure* (Englewood Cliffs, N. J.: Prentice-Hall, Inc., 1964), pp. 109, 110.

Following the Witnesses' reasoning to a logical conclusion, the above facts would argue that the "time of the end" began *before* 1914!

2. *"Disobedient to parents," "Lovers of money," "Lovers of pleasures rather than lovers of God," "Having a form of godly devotion but proving false to its power."* The *Awake!* issue of October 8, 1968 (pp. 10, 11) presents the foregoing under four points as signs of the "last days." The reference from which these are drawn is II Timothy 3:2-5. In an article of some length in the May 1, 1899 *Watch Tower,* this passage, including verse 1 is quoted and explained. The discussion is introduced with the statement:

> Claiming, as we do, that we are now living in the closing days of the Gospel age, it is quite proper that we should look about us to see whether or not present conditions correspond to the Apostle's inspired descriptions of what must be expected in the last days of this age.[63]

Each portion of the passage is examined and viewed as being fulfilled at that time:

> Having satisfied ourselves respecting the fulfilment of the Apostle's charges against "Christendom" and having found his predictions fully corroborated by facts well witnessed to, the question arises, Can the Lord's truly consecrated people learn any further valuable lessons and what are they?[64]

Corroboration of the fulfillment of this prophecy is drawn from contemporary sources: the Governor of the State of New Hampshire and the Methodist *Epworth Herald.* If this Timothy passage seemed to apply so well in the 1890's, it is difficult to see how the same passage can be used to prove that this world has been in the "last days" only since 1914.

3. *"Men Becoming Faint Out of World-wide Fear."* This sign is based on Luke 21:26. That this verse had fulfillment before 1914 to Russell and Society writers is clear. It is applied by Russell to that which he observed in 1879:

> ... Today every civilized nation is in dread, and Nihilism, Communism and Socialism, are household words, and we see "men's hearts failing for fear and for looking after those things *coming* on the earth,

---

[63] *Watch Tower Reprints,* III, p. 2459.
[64] *Ibid.,* p. 2463.

for the powers of heaven (governments) shall be shaken." Luke xxi. 26.[65]

In 1882, J. C. Sunderlin also saw fulfillment of Luke 21:26:

> It is a *fact*, not an *assumption*, but a solemn fact, that we are *now* living in a time when crime and *corruption* have assumed prodigious proportions.... Even all the machinery of church and state seems to be so rotten that many are exclaiming, without knowledge that their utterances are the fulfillment of the spirit of prophecy: "I don't know what we are coming to!" Thus already their hearts are beginning to "fail them for fear, and for looking after those things which are coming on the earth." (Luke 21:26)[66]

4. *"Increased Lawlessness."* In the May, 1882 *Watch Tower* it is reported that "a late secular paper of some note said that crimes were *becoming* so frequent that they, in their weekly issue, could only make a *statement* of them, not having room for particulars."[67]

5. *"This Good News of the Kingdom Will Be Preached...."* (NWT) Based on Matthew 24:14, the sign as stated in *Make Sure of All Things* adds to the Scripture: "World-wide Preaching of the Established Kingdom as Good News" (p. 338). The Witnesses currently quote their own works and other publications to indicate that they have covered the earth with their witnessing and thereby fulfilled Matthew 24:14. Russell proclaimed that the fulfillment had already been realized in the nineteenth century:

> The text says nothing about how the testimony will be received. This witness has already been given. In 1861 the reports of the Bible Societies showed that the Gospel had been published in every language of earth, though not all of earth's millions had received it. No, not one half of the fourteen hundred millions living have ever heard the name of Jesus. Yet the condition of the text is fulfilled: the gospel has been preached in all the world for a *witness*–to every *nation*.[68]

Eleven years later Russell again confirmed the fulfillment of Matthew 24:14:

---

[65] *Watch Tower Reprints*, I (September, 1879), p. 26.

[66] *Watch Tower Reprints*, I (May, 1882), p. 353.

[67] *Ibid.*, p. 352.

[68] *The Divine Plan of the Ages* (Brooklyn: Watch Tower Bible and Tract Society, 1886), pp. 91, 92.

This *witness* has already been given: the word of the Lord, the gospel of the Kingdom, has been published to every nation of earth. Each individual has not heard it; but that is not the statement of the prophecy. It was to be, and has been, a national proclamation. And *the end has come!*[69]

6. *"Nations Confused and Perplexed as to Course."* This sign is based upon Luke 21:25. In May, 1882, one is told:

No sane man today, unless he is trying to sustain a creed, fails to see (recognize) that thrones stand unsteady, and that throughout the world there is a feeling of *distrust* among all classes; there is *"perplexity."* Luke 21:25. Verily, the foundations of the earth *do shake.*[70]

7. *"Separating the People of the Nations into 'Sheep' and 'Goats.'"* In an article entitled "The Presence of the Son of Man," published in 1910, the reader is informed that

some very earnest Bible students believe that we are in this harvest period now; that the Son of Man, the glorious Messiah, invisible to men, is even now present doing a searching and separating work in his church ....[71]

8. *"Instability and Insecurity World-wide Despite Claims of Leaders."* References quoted in connection with this sign are Jeremiah 6:14 and Ezekiel 13:10, 11. Both passages emphasize the saying of peace when there is no peace. Six pages of the book *The Battle Armageddon* (1897) are given to the development of this very theme, "The Cry of 'Peace! Peace! When There Is No Peace'" (pp. 150-156). "Such a proclamation, participated in by all the nations of Christendom was that which was issued from the great naval display on the occasion of the opening of the Baltic canal."[72]

9. *"Many Will Ridicule Sign Though Evidence Conclusive."* While applied by the present Witnesses to the 1914 "time of the end," it was applied by Russell to those who would scoff during the presence of Christ, according to his view 1874-1914.[73]

10. *"Men Seek Relief in Makeshift Organizations, Clubs, Institutions."* This sign is based on Revelation 6:15-17. Russell

---

[69] *The Battle of Armageddon*, p. 568.

[70] *Watch Tower Reprints*, I, p. 353.

[71] *Watch Tower Reprints*, V (November 1, 1910), p. 4706.

[72] *The Battle of Armageddon*, p. 151.

[73] *The Time Is at Hand*, pp. 167, 170.

explains this passage as realizing fulfillment in the late nineteenth century (1889):

> The real fulfilment is already beginning: the great, the rich, and no less the poor, are seeking to the mountains and rocks and caves for shelter from the darkening storm of troubles which all see is gathering.[74]

If space permitted, each of the thirty-nine signs could be dealt with as has been done with the above ten. Several conclusions may be stated at this point: (1) None of these signs permit an establishing of a particular date for the beginning of the "time of the end." (2) The signs seem so general that they can be applied just as well to the nineteenth century as to the twentieth. (3) Would it not be just as logical to date the beginning of the "time of the end" in the 1940's after the conflict of World War II? Or one could select some other date, such as 1967 when the city of Jerusalem was liberated from foreign control by the six-day war (June 5-10).

---

[74] *Ibid.*, p. 139.

Chapter 4

AN EXAMINATION AND REFUTATION OF THE WITNESSES' POSITION ON THE 1975 CHRONOLOGY

The Witness writers who stated that their chronology established that 6,000 years since Adam's creation would end in 1975, did not claim infallibility, but they did say that this calculation was "reasonably accurate."[1] In the mind of the average Witness there was little or no doubt that the date was correct. This conclusion was drawn by the writer from his conversations with individual Jehovah's Witnesses. The same impression was reported by Ruth Brandon in her article, "Jehovah 1975": "For the Witness, there's no question of 'if.' Armageddon *will* happen in 1975, if not earlier, and the only important thing in this life is what's going to happen then, in the next."[2]

Several important subjects are considered in this chapter: (1) the 6,000-year tradition, (2) the expressions of certainty concerning the Witnesses' current chronology and particulars which must be considered in connection with the establishment of a chronology, and (3) problems which require the rejection of the Witnesses' chronological system.

I. THE WITNESSES AND THE 6,000-YEAR TRADITION

The view that 6,000 years of human existence would be followed by God's intervention and the end of the present world system can be traced through "pagan, Jewish, Christian and Mohammedan theology."[3]

---

[1] *The Watchtower*, LXXXIX (August 15, 1968), p. 499.

[2] *New Society* (August 7, 1969), p. 202.

[3] Arnold D. Ehlert, *A Bibliographic History of Dispensationalism* (Grand Rapids: Baker Book House, 1965), p. 8. Ehlert credits D. T. Taylor "for citing a large part of the literature dealing with the six and seven thousand year tradition . . . in his book, *The Voice of the Church.*"

The 6,000 year view can be found in a number of pagan sources. These include: Chaldean, Egyptian, Etruscan, Median and Persian writings, the Sibylline Oracles and the philosopher Zoroaster.[4]

"A Jewish tradition of the six thousand years, followed by the Sabbath millennium, dates at least from the second century B.C. . . ."[5] The view is found in the Midrash, the *Cespar Mishna* and *Gemarah.*[6]

Within Christianity the tradition is found at least as early as the *Epistle of Barnabas* (A.D. 70-79). Church Fathers who are quoted by Ehlert as they state the position include: Justin Martyr (c. 100-163/67), Irenaeus (c. 130-?), Hippolytus (3rd. cent.), Cyprian (c. 200-258), Lactantius (c. 260-340), Jerome (c. 349?-420), Hilary, Bishop of Poitiers (c. 300-367), Augustine (354-430), Andrew of Crete (died c. 699) and Ambrose Ansbert (8 cent.).[7] Other names of the old Fathers could be given.[8]

It is interesting to note that following the chronology of the Septuagint many early writers concluded that *they* were living in the end of the age.

> Elliott in his *Horae Apocalypticae,* lists the following dates for the close of the sixth millennium, and the ushering in of the seventh, as set by some of the ancients: Sibylline Oracles, c. A.D. 196 (the earliest); Cyprian, c. 243; Hippolytus, 500; Lactantius, c. 500; Constantius, c. 500; Hilarion, 500; Sulpitius Severus 581; and Augustine, 650.[9]

The 6,000 year tradition was taught quite extensively during the middle ages and afterwards into the eighteenth century. Writers who taught the view include, Joachim Abbas (?-1212?), Jean Pierre d'Olive (1248/49-1298), Melanchthon (1487-1560), Joseph Mede (1586-1638), John Bunyan (1628-1688) and Robert Fleming (?-1716).[10]

A number of writers and movements propagated the six thousand year system during the nineteenth century. Among them were William Miller and the Second Adventists. Pastor Russell credited Bowen of England for first digging out the

---

[4] *Ibid.,* pp. 8-10.
[5] *Ibid.,* p. 10.
[6] *Ibid.,* p. 11.
[7] *Ibid.,* pp. 12-19.
[8] *Ibid.,* p. 19. See Appendix B.
[9] *Ibid.*
[10] *Ibid.,* p. 21.

correct 6,000 year chronology. This source is acknowledged in the *Watch Tower* of October/November 1881.

> We do not here give the time arguments or proofs. They are familiar to many, and can be had in more convenient shape. We merely notice here that the Bible chronology, first dug from Scripture by Bowen of England, which shows clearly and positively that the 6,000 years from Adam ended in 1873, and consequently that there the morning of the Millennial day (the seventh thousand) began, in which a variety of things are due.[11]

That Russell borrowed from the Adventists is also evident.

> I recalled certain arguments used by my friend Jonas Wendell and other Adventists to prove that 1873 would witness the burning of the world, etc.—the chronology of the world showing that the six thousand years from Adam ended with the beginning of 1873—and other arguments drawn from the Scriptures and supposed to coincide.[12]

Russell also explained how Second Adventist, N. H. Barbour, convinced him that the 1873 date for the end of the 6,000 years and the second presence of Christ in 1874 were correct.[13]

The 6,000 year chronology as "dug from Scripture" by Bowen, propagated by Second Adventists, and followed by Russell is still the basic chronology of the Jehovah's Witnesses today—with one major adjustment, the acceptance of the reading of "four hundred and eightieth year" at I Kings 6:1 instead of the emendation to "five hundred and eightieth year" accepted by Russell.[14]

---

[11] *Watch Tower Reprints*, I, p. 289. The reference to "Bowen of England" could be Thos. Bowen. Other writers of the nineteenth century placed the termination of the 6,000 years at different dates. R. C. Shimeall placed the end of the period at 1868 in his book *Our Bible Chronology* (New York: A. S. Barnes and Burr, 1859), p. 182. E. B. Elliott stated that Fynes Clinton's chronology had the 6,000 years since Adam end in 1862. Elliott ended the period in 1865, *Horae Apocalypticae* (fourth ed.; London: Seeleys, 1851), IV, pp. 228, 235. Elliott also includes C. Bowen's chronology, that followed by Russell (p. 236).

[12] *Watch Tower Reprints*, IV (July 15, 1906), p. 3822.

[13] *Ibid.*

[14] Compare *Watch Tower Reprints*, III (May 15, 1896), p. 1980 and *The Time Is at Hand* (Allegheny, Pa.: Watch Tower Bible and Tract Society, 1889), p. 53, with *The Truth Shall Make You Free*, p. 150. Russell figured the period from Solomon's death to Zedekiah's overthrow as 393 years, but the present position finds only 390.

Russell, following Bowen's chronology and that of the Second Adventists with which he had contact, placed Adam's creation at 4128 B.C., with a period of two years spent in the Garden of Eden. Adam's innocence was ended by the fall in 4126 B.C. Current Watchtower chronology places the creation of Adam at 4026 B.C., but reduces the time in the Garden to "weeks or months," ("or years" was added in the October 1, 1975 *Watchtower*, p. 579).

62   THE JEHOVAH'S WITNESSES AND PROPHETIC SPECULATION

Russell placed the acceptance of the 6,000 year prophetic scheme in proper perspective when he wrote:

> And though *the Bible contains no direct statement* that the seventh thousand will be the epoch of Christ's reign, the great Sabbath Day of restitution to the world, yet the *venerable tradition* is not without reasonable foundation [italics mine].[15]

This statement, published in 1889, is just as accurate today as it was at that time. The admission that "the Bible contains no direct statement" that anything was to happen after 6,000 years and that the idea was based on "venerable tradition" should be pondered by anyone who claims that prophetic teaching must be based on the Bible.

II. THE WITNESSES AND BIBLICAL CHRONOLOGY

Confidence in a "correct" chronology. To the uninformed or uncritical reader, the articles and other treatments which have dealt with chronology in recent Watchtower publications look impressive and exude confidence. The reader is informed that that which is presented is "reliable" and "trustworthy," the result of earnest and independent research of the Bible.[16] One Witness writer writes boldly:

> One thing is absolutely certain, Bible chronology reinforced with fulfilled Bible prophecy shows that six thousand years of man's existence will soon be up, yes, within this generation! (Matt. 24:34)[17]

It is significant that Russell's chronology, which established the creation of Adam as 4128 B.C., rather than the current date of 4026, was also verified by elaborate "proofs" and viewed as trustworthy. Some illustrations of this follow.

In the book *Three Worlds,* published in 1877, the reader is informed that "the mass of evidence which synchronizes with the fact that the six thousand years are already ended, is absolutely startling, to one who will take the trouble to investi-

---

[15] *The Time Is at Hand,* p. 39.

[16] *Life Everlasting—in Freedom of the Sons of God* (Brooklyn: Watchtower Bible and Tract Society, 1966), pp. 28, 29; *Awake!,* XLVII (October 8, 1966), p. 19; *The Watchtower,* XC (October 15, 1969), p. 622.

[17] *The Watchtower,* LXXXIX (August 15, 1968), p. 500.

gate," and that "clear proof can be found that the six thousand years from Adam are ended."[18]

The November 15, 1904 *Zion's Watch Tower* contained four diagrams submitted by three supporters of Russell's chronology. Russell explained the significance of these studies:

> Each has peculiarities of its own, yet all show *parallels* additional to those presented in DAWN, Vol. 2, and all serve the one purpose of confirming the chronology presented in that volume, as the only possible and consistent Bible chronology, on which alone all the various lines of prophecy are harmonizable . . . .
>
> The lesson of the accompanying diagrams is that no such *parallels* would be possible were a single one of our prominent dates altered. For instance, the two years' difference between the end of the 6,000 years, 1872 A.D. and the beginning of the antitypical Jubilee period, 1874 A.D. . . .
>
> . . . .
>
> Do not these dove-tailing figures prove (as nearly as faith could expect proof) that we are right respecting the chronology on which these matters are based . . . ?[19]

In the June 15, 1905 *Zion's Watch Tower* there is an extended article by J. Edgar entitled, "Remarkable Chronological Parallels." This article contains "Three charts of history, showing various parallels, all confirmatory of our chronological applications." At the end of the article there is yet another outline chart, this one prepared by U. G. Lee, which again demonstrates parallels which "prove" that the 6,000 years ran out in 1874.[20]

Many additional pages are given over to supposed reliability of the old chronology by Russell and such dates as 1874 and 1878.[21]

In the 1917 publication, *The Finished Mystery*, Pastor Russell's chronology is said to be further corroborated by the Great Pyramid of Egypt.

> Morton Edgar, author of *Pyramid Passages*, has found foreshown in the Great Pyramid of Egypt abundant evidence of the accuracy of the Bible chronology of Pastor Russell and the supplements thereto sup-

---

[18] Barbour and Russell, *Three Worlds, and the Harvest of this World*, pp. 67, 186.

[19] *Watch Tower Reprints*, IV (November 15, 1904), pp. 3459, 3460. See Appendix C.

[20] *Ibid.*, p. 3579. See Appendix C.

[21] See *The Time Is at Hand*, Chapter VII, pp. 201-245.

plied by Dr. John Edgar, deceased.... Pastor Russell's chronology was written before he ever saw the pyramid....

The chronology as it appears in the STUDIES IN THE SCRIPTURES is accurate....[22]

The Society, still convinced of the accuracy of its chronology, published the following in 1922:

> It is on the basis of such and so many correspondencies—in accordance with the soundest laws known to science—that we affirm that, *Scripturally, scientifically, and historically, present-truth chronology is correct beyond a doubt.* Its reliability has been abundantly confirmed by the dates and events of 1874, 1914, and 1918. Present-truth chronology is a secure basis on which the consecrated child of God may endeavor to search out things to come.
>
> ... Many years ago all these matters were deeply considered by Pastor Russell, and he declared, in an article that we will soon republish, that a change of one year would destroy the entire system of chronology.[23]

It is history that this chronology which was stated to be *"correct beyond a doubt"* was rejected for that which is presently accepted. It was in 1943, with the publication of *The Truth Shall Make You Free,* that a new creation chronology, replacing the old was published. A careful reading of the chapter entitled, "The Count of Time," reveals that there is absolutely no mention of the old time reckoning.[24]

Chronology based on supposition and faith. In an article in *Zion's Watch Tower* Russell cautioned his readers concerning Bible chronology. Under the subheading "Chronology Based Upon Faith" he stated:

> ... We have pointed out there that the chronology of the Bible is not stated with great clearness, that fractions of years are ignored and that there are certain breaks in it.
>
> We have suggested that ordinarily the chronology would be *quite insufficient as evidence and that our acceptance of it is based on faith—on the supposition that God wished to give us a chronology,* wished that we might have some knowledge of the times and seasons,

---

[22] Clayton J. Woodworth and George H. Fisher (eds.) (1926 ed.; Brooklyn: Peoples Pulpit Association, 1917), pp. 60, 61. See Appendix A.

[23] *The Watch Tower,* XLIII (June 15, 1922), p. 187.

[24] Pp. 141-152.

and yet wished that it might be so obscure and indefinite as to *require faith* on the part of his people [italics mine].[25]

Under the title "Knowledge and Faith Regarding Chronology" a question from a reader of *Zion's Watch Tower* is presented and answered.

> A dear Brother inquires, Can we feel absolutely sure that the Chronology set forth in the DAWN-STUDIES is correct?—that the harvest began in A.D. 1874 and will end in A.D. 1914 in a world-wide trouble which will overthrow all present institutions and be followed by the reign of righteousness of the King of Glory and his bride, the church?
> ... Our claim has always been that they [calculations] are based on *faith*....
>
> ....
>
> ... Thus we sought to prove that chronology cannot be built on *facts*, but can be received only on faith....[26]

In another article Russell wrote: "As stated in DAWN, Vol. II, the Bible Chronology presents a sufficiency of difficulties to require *faith that God meant to give us a time measurement.*"[27]

Two thoughts clearly emerge from Russell's quotations: (1) One must *assume* that God wished to give a creation and eschatalogical chronology in the Bible. (2) A chronology derived from the Bible must be accepted on the *basis of faith.* The emphases on supposition and faith are not found in the current publications of the Jehovah's Witnesses, although the basis for their chronology has not changed since Russell's time.

Most Bible scholars of the twentieth century reject the attempts at establishing a complete and meaningful chronology on the basis of information in the Bible. The following statement illustrates the point:

> Still another difficulty arises from the using of the genealogies of the Bible as a basis for chronology. Many chronologies have been constructed upon the assumption that the genealogies might be so used. The careful scrutiny of the genealogies and the use made, or not made, of them in the Bible reveals that they may never be so used as a means of constructing a chronology.[28]

---

[25] *Watch Tower Reprints,* VI (May 1, 1914), p. 5450.

[26] *Watch Tower Reprints,* V (October 1, 1907), p. 4067.

[27] *Watch Tower Reprints,* IV (November 15, 1904), p. 3459.

[28] Edward Mack, "Chronology of the Old Testament," *International Standard Bible Encyclopedia* (1939), I, p. 644A.

Chronology and the creation date. Pastor Russell and many others in the past have attempted to calculate the date of Adam's creation on the basis of the data in the Bible. Each felt that his particular scheme was correct. The same is true for the Watchtower Society today. Both Russell and the present Society acknowledged that other attempts had been made and these had failed. The Pastor referred to "between one and two hundred different systems"[29] and a recent *Watchtower* issue reported that

> a hundred years ago when a count was taken, no less than 140 different timetables had been published by serious scholars. In such chronologies the calculations as to when Adam was created vary all the way from 3616 B.C.E. to 6174 B.C.E. with one wild guess set at 20,000 B.C.E.[30]

With so many studies "by serious scholars" with such diverse results, one might question whether a valid chronology was either possible or intended in Scripture. It also should be pointed out that the quotations above do not reflect the full measure of the problem as the statements which follow demonstrate.

Joseph Packard published the following in 1858:

> The uncertainty of ancient chronology and the want of agreement among chronologists have passed into a proverb. Scaliger complains that no two systems could be found to agree, and that he rose from the study more doubtful than ever.
>
> ....
> ... We are sorry to damp sanguine hopes of success in the attainment of certainty in this science; but when we remember that Sir Isaac Newton spent a great part of the last thirty years of his life in this study, and wrote over his system *sixteen* times [footnote: Whiston in his life says that Sir Isaac wrote out *eighteen* copies with his own hand, differing slightly from each other.] without settling the disputed points, and that this subject has exercised the great minds of Usher, Scaliger, and Playfair, without much success, we dare not hope that where they have failed, others will succeed. As long as we are deficient in historical and chronological data, so long the difficulty will remain.
>
> ... We have spoken of the want of agreement among chronologists. In proof of it we might mention that there are on record no less than *three hundred* different opinions as to the era of the creation, their greatest difference being no less than 3268 years.[31]

---

[29] *Watch Tower Reprints*, I (December, 1883), p. 561.

[30] LXXXIX (August 15, 1968), pp. 494, 495.

[31] "Sacred Chronology," *Bibliotheca Sacra*, XV (April, 1858), pp. 289, 290.

In the *Encyclopaedia Britannica* treatment on "Chronology" in the 1892 edition W. L. R. Cates wrote:

> Des Vignoles, in the preface to his *Chronology of Sacred History*, asserts that he collected upwards of two hundred different calculations the shortest of which reckons only 3483 years between the creation of the world and the commencement of the vulgar era, and the longest 6984. The difference amounts to thirty-five centuries.[32]

In the article on "Chronology" in the *Catholic Encyclopedia* (1908) the writer J. A. Howlett referred to the confusion at that time:

> In an article on Biblical chronology it is hardly necessary in these days to discuss the date of creation. At least 200 dates have been suggested, varying from 3483 to 6934 years B.C., all based on the supposition that the Bible enables us to settle the point. But it does nothing of the sort.[33]

The article on "Old Testament Chronology" in the *International Standard Bible Encyclopedia* reflects the problem:

> The ancient Oriental world did not think epochally and so the epochal method of recording history has no place in their record. It is no wonder that the attempt to put an epoch into the Biblical record meets with such difficulty as that no two chronologists agree, and no two editions of the same chronology, while the author is still alive and able to revise his work.[34]

This writer has located scores of similar expressions as recorded above. These may be found by the reader in many of the standard Bible dictionaries and commentaries. Typical of the statements of contemporary authors on Bible chronology are the observations by E. R. Thiele:

> The chronology of the Old Testament presents many complex and difficult problems. The data are not always adequate or clear, and at times are almost completely lacking. Because of insufficient data many of the problems are at present beyond solution. Even where the data are abundant the exact meaning is often not immediately apparent, leaving scope for considerable difference of opinion and giving rise to many variant chronological reconstructions. The chronological problem is thus one of the availability of evidence, of the correct evaluation and

---

[32] V, p. 713.
[33] III, p. 731.
[34] Mack, p. 644A.

68 THE JEHOVAH'S WITNESSES AND PROPHETIC SPECULATION

interpretation of that evidence, and of its proper application. Only the most careful study of all the data, both Biblical and extra-Biblical, can hope to provide a satisfactory solution.

. . . .

Because of the difficulties involved, it must be admitted that the construction of an absolute chronology from Adam to Abraham is not now possible on the basis of the available data.[35]

In preparation for this book a number of publications were examined, many of which presented dates for the creation of Adam. The table which follows is a sampling of the dates proposed by various writers. It is interesting to note that the problem of Old Testament chronology and speculation as to the date of Adam's creation are still subjects of lively debate.

PROPOSED DATES FOR THE CREATION OF ADAM

Date B.C.	Author	Copyright or Publication Date of Source[36]
3958	Selwyn	1899
3983	Petavius, cited by Poole	1863
3996	Totten	1892
4000	Van Lennep, Davidson	1928, 1957
4003	Panin	----
4046	Mauro	1922
4100	Armstrong	1971
4125	Waring	1935
4132	Shimeall	1859
4172	M'Clintock and Strong	1868
c. 4970	Whitelaw	1970
5100	Hartman	1971
5300	Auchincloss	1908
5361	Poole	1863
5394	A. Rutherford, cited by Smith	1957
5407	A. Rutherford	1971

---

[35] "Chronology, Old Testament" *The Zondervan Pictorial Bible Dictionary* (second ed.; Grand Rapids: Zondervan Publishing House, 1963), p. 166. See also: K. A. Kitchen, *Ancient Orient and Old Testament* (Chicago: Inter-Varsity Press, 1966), pp. 35-78.

[36] The copyright or publication dates do not in every case represent the year that date for the creation of Adam was first published.

5411	Hales, cited by Totten	1892
5421	Poole	1863
5426	Jackson, cited by Poole	1863
5546	Akers	1855
5556	Rehwinkle	1966
5654	Teachout	1971
5862	Rimmer	1929
11,013	H. Camping	1970

WATCHTOWER PROPOSED DATES FOR THE CREATION OF ADAM

Date B.C.	Watchtower Source	Copyright date
4129	*Watch Tower Reprints*, p. 1980	1896
4128	Russell, *The Time Is at Hand*, p. 53	1889
4028	*The Truth Shall Make You Free*, p. 152	1943
4026	*The Kingdom Is at Hand*, p. 171	1944
4025	*New Heavens and a New Earth*, p. 364	1953
4026	*All Scripture Is Inspired of God and Beneficial*, p. 286	1963

Can Adam's creation date be determined on the basis of Scripture as the Witnesses and others have claimed? An examination of the numerous systems and differing results of each would cause the informed and objective scholar to answer in the negative. This writer's sentiments are well expressed by Fred Kramer:

> In our evaluation of the method of computing chronology on the basis of genealogy, as employed by Ussher and others, we have come to the conclusion that the method is wrong and unsupported by the Scripture itself. We cannot fail to note that the purpose of the genealogies in Scriptures is something far other than the computation of chronology.[37]

An invalid method of computing chronology cannot yield other than invalid and confusing conclusions.

Adam's stay in the Garden. Although the Watchtower Society leadership condemns speculation on the part of the individual Jehovah's Witness, it has been obvious, and will be

---
[37] "A Critical Evaluation of the Chronology of Ussher," *Rock Strata and the Bible Record*, ed. Paul A. Zimmerman (St. Louis: Concordia Publishing House, 1970), pp. 62, 63.

more so, that speculation is a characteristic of Watchtower writers.[38] The question of Adam's length of stay in the Garden of Eden is important, because this time is not considered by the Witnesses as part of the "seventh day" and therefore must be subtracted from the 5996 years which they calculate have elapsed as of 1971. This would make the 6,000 years run out later.

The time Adam spent in the Garden after his creation, before the fall, is not stated in Scripture. Russell speculated that the time which elapsed was two years:

> ... Just how long we are not informed, but two years would not be an improbable estimate....
>
> Recalling all these circumstances, we can scarcely imagine that a shorter time than two years elapsed in that sinless condition . . . .[39]

It is enlightening to read Witness writers who argue for contradictory positions on the basis of their current thinking. As an example, *The Watchtower* issue of February 1, 1955 argues (while not stating a definite period such as Russell's two years) that the 6,000 years would not run out exactly in keeping with the chronology

> because Adam lived some time after his creation in the latter part of Jehovah's sixth creative period, before the seventh period, Jehovah's sabbath began.
>
> Why, it must have taken Adam *quite some time to name all the animals,* as he was commissioned to do. Further, it appears from the *New World Translation* that, even while Adam was naming the animals, other family kinds of living creatures were being created for Adam to designate by name. (Gen. 2:19, footnote d, NW) It was not until after Adam completed this assignment of work that his helpmate Eve was created... [italics mine].
>
> The very fact that, as part of Jehovah's secret, no one today is able to find out how much time Adam and later Eve lived during the closing days of the sixth creative period, so no one can now determine when six thousand years of Jehovah's present rest day come to an end.[40]

In *The Watchtower* of August 15, 1968, although Adam's

---

[38] *The Watchtower,* LXXIII (February 1, 1952), pp. 80-82.

[39] *Thy Kingdom Come,* pp. 127, 128.

[40] *The Watchtower,* LXXVI (February 1, 1955), p. 95.

time in the Garden of Eden is stated as an "unknown amount," it is shortened:

> And yet the end of that sixth creative "day" could end within the same Gregorian calendar year of Adam's creation. *It may involve only a difference of weeks or months, not years.*
>
> ....
>
> ... So the lapse of time between Adam's creation and the end of the sixth creative day, *though unknown,* was a comparatively short period of time [italics mine].[41]

Whereas in the 1955 *Watchtower* the naming of the animals is stated to have taken "quite some time," the 1968 *Watchtower* interpretation speculates that "the naming of the animals by Adam, and his discovery that there was no complement for himself, required no great length of time." The earlier rendition which stated that the *New World Translation* showed that animals were created after Adam's creation is also rejected in the 1968 explanation: "This does not mean that the animals and birds were created after Adam was created. Genesis 1:20-28 shows it does not mean that."[42]

The estimate of two years by Russell, no definite number of years by the second Witness, and the recent conclusion of "weeks or months, not years" for Adam's stay in the Garden are *pure speculation.*

A very important question comes to mind. Why did it take God almost 7,000 years (according to the Witnesses' view of the creative "days") to create what came into existence on the sixth "day," and only take a matter of "weeks or months" for Adam's creation and the associated events? Is it not legitimate to see Adam's creation, work and presence in the Garden of Eden as something which could take *many years* on the basis of a 7,000-year "day"?

What makes a stay of "weeks or months" more reasonable than two, three, five, ten, twenty or more years for the period? Since it is admitted that there is *no place in the Bible* where one can learn how long Adam was in the Garden, any time set would be nothing more than guess work. If the Witnesses' dates in the future are based on such speculation, they too must be viewed as pure theory and not as fact.

---

[41] LXXXIX, pp. 499, 500.
[42] *Ibid.*

III. THE WITNESSES AND BIBLICAL GENEALOGIES

The problem of sources. The Witnesses have based their chronology of the Patriarchs on the genealogies of Genesis 5 and 11 as recorded in the Hebrew text without giving value to other ancient texts. But as the accompanying Table shows, a comparison of the available sources displays some significant differences in the figures given for the partriarchs in these chapters. While the present writer is in agreement with the Witnesses and most Bible scholars today that the Masoretic text is superior to the *Septuagint* and Samarian Pentateuch in accuracy, Thiele states that

> an endeavor to assess the relative values of the three sources involved accomplishes little, for the indications are that none is altogether complete. Certainly the LXX had great weight in NT times, for in Luke's table of the ancestor's of Christ, there is listed a second Cainan, son of Arphaxad (Luke 3:36), in harmony with the LXX of Gen. 11:12, 13—a name not found in the MT.[43]

Theodore L. Handrich further reminds the reader

> that one cannot entirely discount the Septuagint where it differs from the Masoretic Hebrew text. The inspired writers of the New Testament and even our Lord Jesus Himself raised the status of the Septuagint very much by frequently quoting from it as well as from the Hebrew Old Testament.[44]

An examination of the sources, then yields two problems: (1) which of the figures in the three sources should be used in the computation of a chronology?, and (2) are any of the sources actually complete? With these two problems confronting the Witnesses or any chronologer, an absolute chronology is impossible. The second of the problems is developed more fully below.

The probability of abridged genealogies. Until the middle of the nineteenth century Old Testament chronology was built almost entirely on the assumption that the genealogies of Genesis 5 and 11 were complete and could be used for chronological purposes. But upon careful study, most scholars today agree that this is not so, because the genealogies have been abridged. An early, oft-quoted and extensive presentation of the

---
[43] Thiele, p. 166.
[44] *The Creation: Facts, Theories, and Faith* (Chicago: Moody Press, 1953), p. 97.

EARLY PATRIARCHAL GENEALOGIES[45]

Name	Age at birth of successor			Balance of life			Total years		
	MT	LXX	Sam. P.	MT	LXX	Sam. P.	MT	LXX	Sam. P.
Adam	130	230	130	800	700	800	930	930	930
Seth	105	205	105	807	707	807	912	912	912
Enosh	90	190	90	815	715	815	905	905	905
Kenan	70	170	70	840	740	840	910	910	910
Mahalalel	65	165	65	830	730	830	895	895	895
Jared	162	162	62	800	800	785	962	962	847
Enoch	65	165	65	300	200	300	365	365	365
Methuselah	187	167	67	782	802	653	868	969	720
Lamech	182	188	53	595	565	600	777	753	653
Noah	500	500	500	450	450	450	950	950	950
Shem	100	100	100	500	500	500		600	
Arpachshad	35	135	135	403	430	303		438	
Kainan		130			330				
Shelah	30	130	130	403	330	303		433	
Eber	34	134	134	430	370	270		404	
Peleg	30	130	130	209	209	109		239	
Reu	32	132	132	207	207	107		239	
Serug	30	130	130	200	200	100		230	
Nahor	29	79	79	119	129	69		148	
Terah	70	70	70				205	205	145

view that abridgment has taken place in Genesis 5 and 11 is that by William H. Green. Green explains his treatment as one which presents

> considerations which seem to me to justify the belief that the genealogies in Genesis v. and xi., were not intended to be used, and cannot properly be used, for the construction of a chronology.
>
> It can scarcely be necessary to adduce proof to one who has even a superficial acquaintance with the genealogies of the Bible, that these are frequently abbreviated by the omission of unimportant names. In fact, *abridgment is the general rule* . . . [italics mine].[46]

A more recent comprehensive presentation of the abridgment

---

[45] R. K. Harrison, *Introduction to the Old Testament* (Grand Rapids: William B. Eerdmans, 1969), p. 150.

[46] "Primeval Chronology," *Bibliotheca Sacra*, XLVII (April, 1890), p. 286. It is

position is found in the *Genesis Flood*. Authors Whitcomb and Morris develop eight "important reasons for questioning the validity of the strict-chronology interpretation of Genesis 11."[47] Since these reasons are important and involved, they are presented in their entirety in Appendix D of the present study. At this point the summarization by Whitcomb and Morris should suffice:

> In summarizing the arguments of this entire discussion, we may say that the lack of an overall total of years for the period from the Flood to Abraham, the absence of Cainan's name and years in the Hebrew text, the symmetrical form of the genealogies of Genesis 5 and 11, the inclusion of data that are irrelevant to a strict chronology, the impossibility of all the post-diluvian patriarchs being contemporaries of Abraham, the Biblical indications of a great antiquity for the judgment of Babel, the fact that the Messianic links were seldom firstborn sons, and the analogy of "begat" being used in he ancestral sense allow the existence of gaps of an undetermined length in the patriarchal genealogy of Genesis 11.[48]

A survey of the other recent articles and books which deal with the subject of Bible chronology reveals that they are in near unanimous agreement that the genealogies of Genesis are not complete. Therefore, they cannot be used as the Witnesses have used them. Yet, from an examination of Watchtower publications, one would never learn that such a view even exists![49] The Society writers may feel that it is best to avoid mention of the abridgment position, for if it is correct, as the evidence indicates, *any* attempt to calculate Adam's creation date on the basis of the Genesis genealogies could *never* be successful!

---

impossible in the space of this book to give the full arguments from the Bible that Green presents in confirming that the genealogies of Genesis 5 and 11 are not complete. The reader is referred to the article which covers pages 285-303. Green stated his conclusion: "... We conclude that the Scriptures furnish no data for a chronological computation prior to the life of Abraham; and that the Mosaic records do not fix and were not intended to fix the precise date either of the Flood or of the creation of the world." (p. 303)

[47] John C. Whitcomb, Jr. and Henry M. Morris, *The Genesis Flood* (Philadelphia: Presbyterian and Reformed Publishing Company, 1961), p. 474.

[48] *Ibid.*, p. 483. See also: *Rock Strata and the Bible Record*, pp. 57-67; Frederick Gardner, "The Chronological Value of the Genealogy in Genesis V," *Bibliotheca Sacra* XXX (April 1873), pp. 323-333.

[49] See the extensive treatment on "Chronology" in *Aid to Bible Understanding* (Brooklyn: Watchtower Bible and Tract Society, 1969), pp. 322-348.

The "second Cainan" of Luke 3:36. Luke, in Chapter 3 of his Gospel, mentions a name in his genealogy which is not found in Genesis 11, the name Cainan. As far as this writer has been able to determine, Russell never considered the problem of Cainan's appearance in this passage. The genealogies of Genesis 11 and Luke 3 at this point are as follows:

Genesis 11:10-18	Luke 3:35, 36 (in part)
Shem	Shem
Arpachshad	Arphaxad
	Cainan
Shelah	Shelah
Eber	Eber
Peleg	Peleg[50]

On the basis of the New Testament manuscripts it must be conceded that the Holy Spirit guided Luke in the recording of this genealogy which adds Cainan, for there is no positive proof of any interpolation in the text at this point.

The Witnesses have attempted to explain away the problem of a separate generation in the following ways: (1) It is stated that Cainan was a "surname of Arphaxad."[51] A footnote in the *New World Translation* on the verse explains that "the name may be a corruption of the word 'Chaldean,' so that the text may have read here: 'the son of the Chaldean Arphaxad.' See Genesis 10:22, 24; I Chronicles 1:17, 18."[52] (2) Or it is argued that "many believe that the name Cainan was not to be found in the original text of Luke's Gospel account."[53] As evidence of this omission, the absence of Cainan's name in the sixth century Cambridge Manuscript (Codex Bezae, designated D) is mentioned.[54]

In answer to the Witnesses' arguments for the deletion of Cainan as a separate generation, it may be remarked. (1) The contention that Cainan may be a corrupted surname and should read "the son of the Chaldean Arphaxad" does not fit the

---

[50] Follows the spellings in the *New World Translation.*
[51] *The Watchtower,* LXXXVI (May 15, 1965), p. 293.
[52] 1963 edition, p. 2993.
[53] *The Watchtower,* LXXXVII (July 1, 1966), p. 416.
[54] *Ibid.*

pattern of the genealogy in this chapter of Luke.[55] (2) It is obvious that Cainan was found in the original Greek text of Luke. Nearly all of the Greek manuscripts of Luke 3:36 have this reading. Therefore, its omission in Codex Bezae is a weak reason for concluding that Cainan was not originally in the text. Its absence in this codex is not unusual, for as Bruce M. Metzger explains:

> No known manuscript has so many and such remarkable variations from what is usually taken to be the normal New Testament text. Codex Bezae's special characteristic is the free addition (and occasionally omission) of words, sentences, and even incidents.[56]

Frederick G. Kenyon characterized Bezae as "undoubtedly the most curious, though certainly not the most trustworthy, manuscript of the New Testament known to us."[57] Moreover, all translations, including the Witnesses', have the reading "Cainan."

Thus, the fact remains that Cainan's name does appear in Luke 3:36, even in the Witnesses' own works; there simply is no solid evidence for its absence in the Greek text. Therefore, it must be allowed that there is *at least one* name omitted in the Masoretic Hebrew text of Genesis 11 and, according to the Septuagint, 130 years must be added to the chronology. This point alone would invalidate the 6,000 year tradition, for 6,000 years would have expired in 1845, rather than 1975!

IV. ADDITIONAL PROBLEMS WITH THE WITNESSES' CHRONOLOGY

Among other problems to be found in the Witnesses' chronology, three additional ones might be mentioned: (1) the dating

---

[55] Plummer points out that throughout the genealogical table the definite article belongs to the name in front of it, since Joseph, the first name has no article before it. Thus, every occurrence of the definite article "means 'who is of,' *i.e.,* either 'the son of' or 'the heir of.' " Alfred Plummer, *A Critical and Exegetical Commentary on the Gospel According to St. Luke,* The International Critical Commentary (fifth ed.; Edinburgh: T. and T. Clark, 1922), p. 105.

The interested reader should examine the way the *New World Translation* (1961 ed.) handles the genealogy (verses 23-38). An examination of the Greek text in the *Kingdom Interlinear Translation of the Greek Scriptures* (Brooklyn: Watchtower Bible and Tract Society, 1969) also supports this author's contention.

[56] *The Text of the New Testament—Its Transmission, Corruption, and Restoration* (New York: Oxford University Press, 1964), p. 50.

[57] *Our Bible and the Ancient Manuscripts* (fourth ed.; London: Eyre and Spottiswoode, 1941), p. 144.

of the Babylonian Captivity, (2) the span of the period between the Divided Kingdom and the fall of Jerusalem, and (3) the date of the Genesis Flood.

The Babylonian Captivity. Figuring backward from the return of the Jews from exile in the autumn of 537 B.C., the Witnesses fit the seventy years of the captivity into the years 607-537 B.C.[58] As the previous chapter has explained, the Witnesses date the fall of Jerusalem 607 B.C. It has been shown that this date deviates from the correct date of 587/6 by twenty years.

From the Dividing of the Kingdom to the Fall of Jerusalem. While it is acknowledged that this period "is one of the more complex periods," the Witnesses find that "a helpful guide as to the overall length of this period of the kings is found in Ezekiel 4:1-7 in the mimic seige of Jerusalem . . . ."[59] Ezekiel's symbolic action, when he was instructed to lie on his left side 390 days and on his right forty are understood by the Witnesses as giving the length of this period as 390 years. "From the division of the kingdom in 997 B.C.E. to the fall of Jerusalem in 607 B.C.E. was 390 years."[60] It may be answered that the starting point for the period is wrong because of the wrong date for the fall of Jerusalem. If the application of the 390 years is correct, the period would be dated 977/6–587/6.

There is a further problem in the use of the Ezekiel passage in as much as the reading "three hundred and ninety" in the Masoretic text is read "one hundred and ninety" in the Septuagint. Charles L. Feinberg remarks that many scholars believe that the latter reading is the correct one.[61] This conclusion is accepted by the translators of *The New English Bible* who place "one hundred and ninety" in the text.

That the period of the Kings from Rehoboam to Zedekiah's fall was a period of 390 years is open to serious question. Thiele and others who have worked out the reigns of the kings of this period have arrived at a lesser total. As K. A. Kitchen explains:

> For the 350 years from Rehoboam of Judah to the fall of Jerusalem in 587 or 586 B.C., some ninety-five per cent of the long series of reigns

---

[58] *Aid to Bible Understanding,* p. 339.

[59] *Ibid.,* p. 338.

[60] *Ibid.*

[61] *The Prophecy of Ezekiel–The Glory of The Lord* (Chicago: Moody Press, 1969), p. 33.

and cross-datings in Kings and Chronicles have been brilliantly worked out by E. R. Thiele—and that not by arbitrary juggling but by full use of proper Ancient Near Eastern procedures, objectively documented.[62]

There are other problems beyond those mentioned herein which question the use and application the Witnesses have made of this passage.[63]

The date of the Genesis Flood. The Witnesses claim that there is "no solid or provable evidence to favor an earlier date than 2369 B.C.E. for the start of the post-Flood human society."[64] This dates the flood, then, at 2370 B.C. By using strictly Bible genealogies (without allowing any gap), Kitchen estimated that the flood would have occurred about 2300 B.C., a date which he found impossible to reconcile with the evidence.

> This date is excluded by the Mesopotamian evidence, because it would fall some 300 or 400 years *after* the period of Gilgamesh or Uruk for whom (in both Epic and Sumerian King List) the Flood was already an event of the distant past. Likewise, the appearing of earliest man (Adam) some 1,947 years or so before Abraham on the Hebrew figures, in about 4000 BC, would seem to clash rather badly with not just centuries but whole millennia of preliterate civilization throughout the Ancient Near East prior to the occurrence of the first written documents just before the First Dynasty in Egypt, c. 3000 BC, and rather earlier in Mesopotamia.[65]

As Whitcomb and Morris add:

> One of the greatest objections to the concept of a geographically universal Deluge in the minds of some scholars today is the fact that there are no historical or archeological evidences for such a vast catastrophe during the third millennium B.C. . . . or even the fourth millennium B.C. . . . Near Eastern cultures apparently have a continuous archeological record (based upon occupation levels and pottery chronology) back to at least the fifth millennium B.C. . . .[66]

---

[62] P. 76. Thiele's dates for the period of Rehoboam to Zedekiah's fall are 931/30-586. Thiele, p. 169.

[63] See Feinberg, pp. 33, 34; Carl F. Keil, *Biblical Commentary on the Prophecies of Ezekiel*, trans. James Martin (Grand Rapids: William B. Eerdman's, 1950), pp. 71-78.

[64] *Aid to Bible Understanding*, p. 334.

[65] Pp. 36, 37. The reader who is interested in studying the background for Kitchen's statement will find ample material cited in the footnotes on these pages of his book.

[66] P. 474.

The above statements present a serious challenge to the proposed chronology of the Watchtower Society.

V. CONCLUSION

A number of important points were considered in the examination and refutation of the Witnesses' 6,000-year chronology. It was found that the 6,000-year theory is not in the Bible, but, as Russell admitted, it is based upon "venerable tradition." It was borrowed from the Second Adventists by Russell and channeled into the Society's thinking by him.

The claims of the Watchtower Society today to have a reliable and trustworthy chronology are extremely questionable—actually impossible, for a number of reasons: (1) The Society made similar claims concerning Russell's chronology, even after his death, and stated as fact that that calculation was *"scripturally, scientifically and historically"* verified as *"correct beyond a doubt."* This chronology was subsequently rejected for that presently accepted. (2) Russell admitted correctly that his (or any other chronology) must be accepted on faith and the "supposition that God wished to give us a chronology." This supposition is rejected by almost all Bible scholars today. (3) On the basis of the hundreds of systems and their various results with regard to the date of Adam's creation (3958 B.C.-11,013 B.C.), it is highly improbable that any date can be accepted as accurate. (4) Since the length of Adam's stay in the Garden is not revealed in the Bible, it was stated that any attempt by the Witnesses to set a time was speculation. Their attempt to set the time as "weeks or months" is just guess work and highly unlikely (if we might be allowed to speculate) in the light of their seven-thousand-year "day." The length of Adam's time in Eden can yield no valid indication as to when the seventh "day" will reach its supposed 6,000 year conclusion. (5) At least three sources for the dating of the early Patriarchal period exist. Many scholars question their completeness and at times it is difficult to determine with assurance which figures are correct. (6) The presence of "second Cainan" in the genealogy of Luke 3:36 introduces another generation into the list of Genesis 11 and, according to the Septuagint reading, 130 extra years. It also opens the door to the possibility, and, as it was shown, the probability of other abridgment of the genealogies of Genesis chapters 5 and 11. (7) That the genealogies were abridged was discussed and the interested reader was referred to Appendix D for actual proof. (8) Lastly, the chronology was called into question on the basis of the Witnesses' approach to the dating of the Babylonian Captivity and the period of the Divided Kingdom. The date for the Flood established by the chronology was shown to be far too late for successful reconciliation with the existing historical and archeological evidence.

An objective study must reject the Witnesses' chronology as scripturally, historically, archeologically and scientifically unsound.

Author's Note
For the Witnesses latest explanations, see pp. 96f.

Chapter 5

THE WITNESSES' POSITION ON THE "LAST DAYS" AND ARMAGEDDON: AN ILLUSION OF URGENCY

The *Los Angeles Herald-Examiner* of July 21, 1969 carried an article with the headline: "ARMAGEDDON DUE IN 70's, WITNESSES TOLD." The paper went on to report:

> Armageddon—The end of the world for all but the Jehovah's Witnesses—is just around the corner, according to Watchtower Society president Nathan H. Knorr who addressed 81,032 Witnesses in the stands and on the playing field yesterday at Dodger Stadium.
>
> Although he did not pinpoint the predicted date, Knorr did narrow it down to the "mid-seventies." The year 1975 has been specifically mentioned in Witness publications.
>
> A spokesman for the Witnesses conceded that they are not as "dogmatic and definite" about the 1975 prediction as they were in proclaiming Armageddon's supposed arrival in 1925.

The significance of 1975 was first stressed in the release on June 25, 1966 of the new book, *Life Everlasting—in Freedom of the Sons of God:*

> ... Six thousand years from man's creation will end in 1975, and the seventh period of a thousand years of human history will begin in the fall of 1975 C.E. ... It would not be by mere chance or accident ... for the reign of Jesus Christ ... to run parallel with the seventh millennium of man's existence.[1]

The date was also emphasized in the *Awake!* of October 8, 1966 in an article entitled, "How Much Longer Will It Be?" (pp. 17-20) The front cover of the October 8, 1968 *Awake!* carries the words: "IS IT LATER THAN YOU THINK?" and in smaller print, "Is time running out for this generation? What

---

[1] (Brooklyn: Watchtower Bible and Tract Society, 1966), pp. 29, 30.

will the 1970's bring?" In the treatment of the subject in the magazine, it ends with the warning:

> You have no time to lose in making friends with God, because time is rapidly running out for this wicked system of things. It is very close to plunging into the chasm of Armageddon. Therefore, take steps quickly to work for survival and for eternal life in God's new order.[2]

It is obvious that the Witnesses and all those who read or study their writings come under a constant pressure of urgency and the reminder that "Armageddon is just around the corner." It is the purpose of this chapter to show that the stress on the "last days" and the threat of Armageddon have been used first by Russell and Rutherford, and then by the Watchtower Society to create an *illusion* of urgency. If anything has been proven over the past more than ninety years, it is that these prophets are certainly false ones—their words have fallen "to the earth" (I Sam. 3:19 NWT; See Deut. 18:20-22).

The statements which have been made over the years in illustration of the above conclusions are presented chronologically in the following development. Similar statements for other years have been located and could be quoted, but those which have been used should suffice.

I. 1877-1899

The following is stated in *Three Worlds*:

> THE END OF THIS WORLD; that is, the end of the *gospel* and the beginning of the *millennial* age is nearer than most men suppose; indeed we have already entered the transition period, which is to be a "time of trouble, such as never was since there was a nation" (Dan. 12:1).[3]
>
> The nations are perplexed, and are preparing for a terrible struggle; huge engines of war are being multiplied by land and sea; millions of men are under arms, and still their numbers are increased, while the people are becoming desperate and alarmed.
>
> When the struggle begins, as soon it must, a ball will be set in motion before which "all the kingdoms of the world, that are upon the face of the earth, shall be thrown down;" and, according to Scripture, one wild scene of desolation and terror will result.[4]

---

[2] XLIX, p. 29.
[3] Barbour and Russell, *Three Worlds, and the Harvest of this World*, p. 17.
[4] *Ibid.*, p. 19.

The January, 1886 *Zion's Watch Tower* began with the observation:

> The outlook at the opening of the New Year has some very encouraging features. The outward evidences are that the marshalling of the hosts for the battle of the great day of God Almighty, is in progress while the skirmishing is commencing.
>
> ....
>
> ... The *time* is come for Messiah to take the dominion of earth and to overthrow the oppressors and corrupters of the earth, (Rev. 19:15 and 11:17, 18) preparatory to the establishment of everlasting peace upon the only firm foundation of righteousness and truth.[5]

In the 1889 publication, *The Time Is at Hand,* the pre-1914 interpretation of prophecy is set forth:

> Be not surprised, then, when in subsequent chapters we present proofs that the setting up of the Kingdom of God is already begun, that it is pointed out in prophecy as due to begin the exercise of power in A.D. 1878, and that the "battle of the great day of God Almighty" (Rev. 16:14.), which will end in A.D. 1914 with the complete overthrow of earth's present rulership, is already commenced. The gathering of the armies is plainly visible from the standpoint of God's Word.[6]

In the observations to open the year 1894 in *Zion's Watch Tower* the reader is informed that "worldly people not only see the great 'battle' approaching, but they see the skirmishing is already beginning all along the line . . . ."[7]

In the July 15, 1894 *Zion's Watch Tower,* under the heading "CAN IT BE DELAYED UNTIL 1914?" Russell wrote:

> Seventeen years ago people said, concerning the time features presented in MILLENNIAL DAWN, They seem reasonable in many respects, but surely no such radical changes could occur between now and the close of 1914: if you had proved that they would come about in a century or two, it would seem much more probable.
>
> What changes have since occurred, and what velocity is gained daily? "The old is quickly passing and the new is coming in."
>
> Now, in view of recent labor troubles and threatened anarchy, our readers are writing to know if there may not be a mistake in the 1914

---

[5] *Watch Tower Reprints,* I, p. 817.

[6] P. 101. The 1915 edition of this text changed the "A.D. 1914" to read "A.D. 1915."

[7] *Watch Tower Reprints,* II (January 1, 1894), p. 1605.

date. They say that they do not see how present conditions can hold out so long under the strain.

We see no reason for changing the figures—nor could we change them if we would. They are, we believe, God's dates, not ours. But bear in mind that the end of 1914 is not the date for the *beginning*, but for the *end* of the time of trouble.[8]

II. 1900-1919

In 1904 Russell stressed the importance of 1910-1912:

According to our expectations the stress of the great time of trouble will be on us soon, somewhere between 1910 and 1912—culminating with the end of the "Times of the Gentiles," October, 1914.

The beginning of the severity of the trouble is not distinctly marked in the Scriptures, and is rather conjectural. We infer that so great a trouble, so world-wide a catastrophe, could scarcely be accomplished in less than three years, and that if it lasted much more than three years "no flesh would be saved."[9]

A number of statements Russell made in 1914, 1915 and 1916 in reference to Armageddon and the establishment of Messiah's Kingdom are significant.

May 1, 1914.

There is absolutely no ground for Bible students to question that the consummation of this Gospel age is now even at the door, and that it will end as the Scriptures foretell in a great time of trouble such as never was since there was a nation. We see the participants in this great crisis banding themselves together . . . . The great crisis, the great clash, symbolically represented as a fire, that will consume the ecclesiastical heavens and the social earth, is very near.[10]

September 1, 1914.

While it is possible that Armageddon may begin next Spring, yet it is purely speculation to attempt to say just when. We see, however, that there are parallels between the close of the Jewish age and this Gospel age. These parallels seem to point to the year just before us—particularly the early months.[11]

---

[8] *Watch Tower Reprints*, II, p. 1677.

[9] *The New Creation* (Brooklyn: Watch Tower Bible and Tract Society, 1904), p. 579.

[10] *Watch Tower Reprints*, VI (May 1, 1914), p. 5450.

[11] *Watch Tower Reprints*, VI (September 1, 1914), p. 5527.

December 14, 1914.

Few of the awakening ones realize that the present war is permitted for the weakening of the nations, preparatory to the utter collapse of the Present Order of things—and the ushering in of the New Order—the Reign of Righteousness, under Messiah's Kingdom.[12]

April 1, 1915.

The Battle of Armageddon, to which this war is leading, will be a great contest between right and wrong, and will signify the complete and everlasting overthrow of the wrong, and the permanent establishment of Messiah's righteous kingdom for the blessing of the world. . . . Our sympathies are broad enough to cover all engaged in the dreadful strife, as our hope is broad enough and deep enough to include all in the great blessings which our Master and his Millennial kingdom are about to bring to the world.[13]

September 1, 1916.

We see no reason for doubting, therefore, that the Times of the Gentiles ended in October, 1914; and that a few more years will witness their utter collapse and the full establishment of God's kingdom in the hands of Messiah.[14]

Sometime during the War.

The present great war in Europe is the beginning of the Armageddon of the Scriptures. (Rev. 16:16-20.) It will eventuate in the complete overthrow of all the systems of error which have so long oppressed the people of God and deluded the world. . . . We believe the present war cannot last much longer until revolution shall break out.[15]

The Finished Mystery stated to be the "POSTHUMOUS WORK OF PASTOR RUSSELL" (p. 2) applies the events formerly scheduled to come in 1914 and before, to the period of 1918-1925. When some of the explanations given in the first edition did not transpire as predicted, a later edition (the edition used was dated 1926) altered the statements and dates. Quotations from this volume with changes noted are given without comment.

. . . The Spring of 1918 will bring upon Christendom a spasm of

---

[12] *New York Times,* December 14, 1914, p. 6.

[13] *Watch Tower Reprints,* VI (April 1, 1915), p. 5659.

[14] *Watch Tower Reprints,* VI (September 1, 1916), p. 5950.

[15] C. T. Russell, *Pastor Russell's Sermons,* p. 676.

anguish greater even than that experienced in the Fall of 1914.... The travail that is coming is to be upon nominal Zion–"Christendom," "Babylon"; and it will be a great and sore affliction–"A Time of Trouble such as was not since there was a nation." (p. 62)

As the fleshly-minded apostates from Christianity, siding with the radicals and revolutionaries, will rejoice at the inheritance of desolation that will be Christendom's after 1918, so will God do to the successful revolutionary movement; it shall be utterly desolated, "even all of it." Not one vestige of it shall survive the ravages of world-wide all-embracing anarchy, in the fall of 1920. (Rev. 11:7-13) [The 1926 ed. reads: "in the end of the time of trouble."] (p. 542)

Pastor Russell's mission, in large part, was to advise Christendom of its impending end, in the time of world-wide trouble. It is the Divine judgment upon the nations.... There will be no chance of escaping from destruction, through the nations .... The trouble is due to the dawning of the Day of Christ, the Millennium. It is the Day of Vengeance, which began in the world war of 1914 and which will break like a furious morning storm in 1918.–Lam. 4:18. (p. 404)

Some interesting developments in connection with the setting up of the Kingdom may occur in 1920, six years after the great Time of Trouble began. It would not be strange if this were so, when we recall that after forty years wandering in the wilderness the Israelites came into possession of the land of Canaan after a further six years. As these matters are still future we can but wait to see. We anticipate that the "earthquake" will occur early in 1918, and that the "fire" will come in the fall of 1920. [Comments on Revelation 11:13. The 1926 ed. reads: "and that the 'fire' will follow in due course."] (p. 178)

This vision of the prophet Ezekiel depicts the established theocratic Kingdom of God on earth, civil and religious, spiritual and earthly.... The Temple ... is a type and symbol of "better things to come," after the wars, revolutions and anarchy of the period from 1914 to 1925 have passed. [The 1926 ed. reads: "of the time of trouble have passed."] (p. 569)[16]

On February 24, 1918 Judge Rutherford "delivered for the first time the lecture that later became entitled 'Millions Now Living Will Never Die.' "[17] This was followed by a "Millions Now Living Will Never Die" campaign from 1918-1921 and a book by the same title.[18] The stage was being set for the new emphasis on 1925.

---

[16] Clayton J. Woodworth and George H. Fisher (eds.), (Brooklyn: People's Pulpit Association, 1917).

[17] *Jehovah's Witnesses in the Divine Purpose*, p. 76.

[18] *Ibid.*, p. 140.

III. 1920-1929

Published late in 1920, Rutherford's *Millions Now Living Will Never Die* booklet and the campaign which promoted it, created quite a stir. The essence of this new stress was that the Kingdom would be set up in 1925.

> Based upon the argument heretofore set forth, then, that the old order of things, the old world, is ending and is therefore passing away, and that the new order is coming in, and that 1925 shall mark the resurrection of the faithful worthies of old and the beginning of reconstruction, it is reasonable to conclude that millions of people now on the earth will be still on the earth in 1925. Then, based upon the promises set forth in the divine Word, we must reach the positive and indisputable conclusion that millions now living will never die.[19]

After the quotation and explanation of Isaiah 35:10, Rutherford looked to the immediate future:

> This is the Golden Age of which the prophets prophesied and of which the Psalmist sang; and it is the privilege of the student of the divine Word today, by the eye of faith, to see that we are standing at the very portals of that blessed time! Let us look up and lift up our heads. Deliverance is at the door![20]

The booklet and the campaign made many new converts, but as 1925 approached Rutherford became less sure of his predictions and by early 1925 he had acknowledged the failure of his expectations.[21]

In 1929, with the publication of *Life,* attention was switched from the 1925 failure to a new issue. The premise of this new book was that the time of the end was very close because the Jews were returning to Palestine.

> If the end of 1925 marks the end of the last fifty-year period, then it follows that we should expect the people to begin to receive some knowledge concerning God's great plan of restoration. The Jews are to have the favors first, and thereafter all others who obey the Lord.[22]

---

[19] (Brooklyn: International Bible Students Association, 1920), p. 97.

[20] *Ibid.,* p. 105.

[21] Timothy White, *A People for His Name* (New York: Vantage Press, 1967), p. 194.

[22] (Brooklyn: Watch Tower Bible and Tract Society), p. 170.

> That the return of the Jews to God's favor means the time when God will extend the privileges of life to the people, both the dead and the living, is shown by the words written [quotes Romans 11:15, 16] ....[23]
>
> That foreshadowed God's purpose now to shortly dash to pieces the Devil's organization that controls all the nations of the earth, and then bring peace and prosperity to the people; and all who obey him will be granted life everlasting on the earth.[24]

The thesis of *Life* was discarded only about a year after its publication.[25]

The year 1929 witnessed two other testimonies to the soon end of the world. One was the publication of the book *Prophecy,* the other was the building of "Beth Sarim" ("House of the Princes") in San Diego. In *Prophecy* Rutherford stated: "Satan knows that shortly he must fight the Lord, and therefore he prepares for the conflict."[26] In concluding the chapter on Armageddon the shortness of the time was again stressed:

> By the proclaiming of the doings of Jehovah and his purposes the people may now know the meaning of the present-day events, and what shall shortly come to pass, and what will be for their good.[27]

"Beth Sarim" was built to provide a place to which the "princes," Abraham, Isaac, Jacob, and others might return just before the closing events of the end. The *San Diego Sun* of March 15, 1930 reported,

> The seven famous men will not have long to rest at their San Diego estate because they soon will lead the forces of the Lord to vanquish the minions of Satan at the Battle of Armageddon, Rutherford believes.

"Beth Sarim" was sold by the Society in 1948.

IV. 1930-1939

The decade, 1930-1939, saw the abandoning of specific date setting, but readers of the Watchtower material were assured

---

[23] *Ibid.,* p. 332.

[24] *Ibid.,* pp. 346, 347.

[25] W. J. Schnell, *Thirty Years a Watch Tower Slave* (Grand Rapids: Baker Book House, 1956), pp. 90, 91.

[26] (Brooklyn: Watch Tower Bible and Tract Society, 1929), p. 266.

[27] *Ibid.,* p. 298.

that the Battle of Armageddon was near. Rutherford explained the new position for this period:

> There was a measure of disappointment on the part of Jehovah's faithful ones on earth concerning the years 1914, 1918 and 1925, which disappointment lasted for a time. Later the faithful learned that these dates were definitely fixed in the Scriptures; and they also learned to quit fixing dates for the future and predicting what would come to pass on a certain date, but to rely (and they do rely) upon the Word of God as to the events that must come to pass.[28]

In *Light*, Volume II, Rutherford wrote, "The great climax is at hand. The kings of earth now set themselves against his anointed Stone."[29] A year later, the first of three volumes of *Vindication* appeared, in which Rutherford warned:

> God's kingdom has begun to operate. His day of vengeance is here, and Armageddon is at hand and certain to fall upon Christendom, and that within an early date. God's judgment is upon Christendom and must shortly be executed.[30]

In his study on the Jehovah's Witnesses, Herbert H. Stroup commented on the continuing importance of the theme of the booklet *Millions Now Living Will Never Die*, even in the early 1930's:

> The theme of the booklet was so rich an energizer of his followers and so compelling an idea in itself that even as late as 1932 Mr. Rutherford was still delivering talks upon it. In that year he declared that the religious work of the Witnesses was "coming to a conclusion," that the end was "only a short time away," and that the end was "much less than the length of a generation."[31]

The book *Salvation* (1939) also stressed the nearness of Armageddon:

> The abundance of Scriptural evidence, together with the physical facts that have come to pass showing the fulfillment of prophecy, conclusively proves that the time for the battle of the great day of God Almighty is very near and that in that battle all of God's enemies shall be destroyed and the earth cleared of wickedness....[32]

---

[28] *Vindication* (Brooklyn: Watch Tower Bible and Tract Society, 1931), I, pp. 338, 339.

[29] (Brooklyn: Watch Tower Bible and Tract Society, 1930), II, p. 327.

[30] I, p. 147.

[31] *The Jehovah's Witnesses* (New York: Columbia University Press, 1945), p. 55.

[32] J. F. Rutherford, (Brooklyn: Watchtower Bible and Tract Society, 1939), p. 310.

Likewise today, all the nations and peoples of earth are face to face with the greatest emergency. They are being warned as God commands, that the disaster of Armageddon is just ahead.[33]

V. 1940-1949

Rutherford's book *Religion* concluded with the chapter "End of Religion" in which he wrote:

> The prophecies of Almighty God, the fulfillment of which now clearly appears from the physical facts, show that the end of religion has come and with its end the complete downfall of Satan's entire organization.[34]
>
> ... The day for final settlement is near at hand.[35]

The year 1940 seemed to be very close to the termination of this "system of things" for Rutherford wrote the following in *The Watchtower:*

> The witness work for THE THEOCRACY appears to be about done in most of the countries of "Christendom." ...
> ... Now the totalitarian rule has suppressed the Theocractic message, and it should be expected that when they quit fighting amongst themselves all the totalitarian rulers will turn their attention to the complete suppression of everything pertaining to the THEOCRATIC GOVERNMENT.
> What, then, does it mean that the THEOCRATIC GOVERNMENT is now suppressed in many nations? It means that the hour is rapidly approaching when the "sign" of Armageddon will be clearly revealed and all who are on the side of Jehovah will see and appreciate it.[36]

Herbert Stroup reported the following incident which occurred shortly before Christmas in 1940. "The wife declared that she would never again celebrate Christmas, but added with a shrug of her shoulders, 'I should worry. The kingdom may be here before Christmas.'"[37]

---

[33] *Ibid.,* p. 361.

[34] (Brooklyn: Watchtower Bible and Tract Society, 1940), p. 336.

[35] *Ibid.,* p. 338.

[36] *The Watchtower,* LXI (September 1, 1940), p. 265.

White (p. 335), quotes from the *1942 Yearbook* (p. 29), completed by Rutherford just before his death: "The record as herewith published would, on the face of it, show that the Theocratic witness work on earth is about done."

[37] P. 142.

In Rutherford's book *Children*, the touching story of two young Jehovah's Witnesses is told. John twenty and Eunice eighteen, who are deeply in love, decided that their marriage should be postponed until after Armageddon and the impending establishment of the Kingdom. John is made to say:

> Armageddon is surely near, and during that time the Lord will clean off the earth everything that offends and is disagreeable.... From now on we shall have our heart devotion fixed on THE THEOCRACY, knowing that soon we shall journey forever together in the earth. Our hope is that within a few years our marriage may be consummated and, by the Lord's grace, we shall have sweet children that will be an honor to the Lord. We can well defer our marriage until lasting peace comes to the earth.[38]

The publication of *The New World*, the first book after Rutherford's death, continued to carry the theme of the closeness of the end and the soon to be realized new world:

> ... THE NEW WORLD IS AT THE DOORS.... The time is short. Those who do not inform themselves and who do not now choose the new world which Higher Powers shall establish will never live to enter into blessings and glories.[39]

In 1943 the book *The Truth Shall Make You Free* warned:

> The final war will come as a most sudden and complete surprise.... Nevertheless, the appearing of the "desolating abomination in the holy place" is an unerring proof that the unknown day and hour of the beginning of the final war is dangerously near.[40]

It was in the same book that the first revised chronology since Russell's was published. Russell's chronology made the 6,000 years since Adam's creation run out in 1872. The new chronology had the same period run out in 1972. The chapter titled "The Count of Time," concluded: "We are therefore near the end of six thousand years of human history, with conditions upon us and tremendous events at hand foreshadowed by those of Noah's day.—Luke 17:26-30."[41]

That this new chronology did establish in the minds of many Witnesses a new date for when Armageddon might take place is

---

[38] (Brooklyn: Watchtower Bible and Tract Society, 1941), p. 366.
[39] (Brooklyn: Watchtower Bible and Tract Society, 1942), p. 10.
[40] P. 341.
[41] *Ibid.*, p. 152.

illustrated by the experience of Marcus Bach with the Witnesses, as reported in 1946. Bach asked a Witness why he sacrificed as he did; the reply and the conversation are given:

> "Armageddon." "Scheduled for when?" "It should come sometime before 1972." He made it sound so commonplace we might have been talking about the weather. And yet, for him, Armageddon would be life's most portentous event.[42]

Bach also records an interesting conversation on children and marriage:

> "Do you have any children?" His answer was sincere but impersonal. "No, we haven't. We think it is better to wait until after Armageddon." ... "Is this a belief among the Witnesses," I asked, "or is it just your idea?" "The Society feels that since the time of the end is so near, people can witness more effectively if they do not have too many responsibilities."[43]

In 1944 the establishment of an "international peace organization" was seen

> as one of the most positive evidences that "the kingdom of heaven is at hand" and that the end of the world arrangement is now near, Jesus foretold the setting up of that anti-christ organization.[44]

In 1946 it was stated that "the disaster of Armageddon, greater than that which befell Sodom and Gomorrah, is at the door."[45]

VI. 1950-PRESENT

It is not necessary to quote extensively from the writings of the period between 1950-1975 to establish that they too stress the nearness of Armageddon. Several examples of statements should suffice.

---

[42] *They Have Found a Faith* (New York: Bobbs-Merrill Company, 1946), p. 34.

[43] *Ibid.*, p. 44. See the same emphasis in the August 7, 1969 issue of *New Society*, p. 201: "Were they planning to have a family out in South America, then? 'No,' said Liz. 'We've decided not to have any children till after Armageddon.'"

[44] *The Kingdom Is at Hand* (Brooklyn: Watchtower Bible and Tract Society, 1944, p. 342.

[45] *Let God Be True* (Brooklyn: Watchtower Bible and Tract Society, 1946), p. 194.

POSITION ON "LAST DAYS" AND ARMAGEDDON

In *This Means Everlasting Life* urgency is stressed:

> Every intelligent creature on earth must determine his own destiny. Now at the consummation of this system of things when the judgment of the nations is under way and the separating of the sheep and the goats with opposite destinies is nearing a conclusion, yes, now is the urgent time to make your determination.[46]

> The march is on! Where? To the field of Armageddon for the "war of the great day of God the Almighty"! God will not hear the unscriptural prayers of all the religious clergy combined on "world prayer" days for the sparing of this old world from Armageddon. It is unavoidable, for Jehovah's time has come to settle definitely the issue of universal sovereignty.[47]

According to the observations of ex-witness Stan Thomas, and other authors as well, the 1953 convention of the Jehovah's Witnesses in Yankee Stadium was of special significance:

> ... the Witnesses were warned to expect an all out attack by Satan's forces (the world) in the near future, an event which would be the spark to ignite Armageddon. As to precisely when this attack was to be expected the Watchtower Society has grown much too wise to officially speculate, but many Witnesses, particularly older ones, felt that 1954 could well be "The Year." After all, Russell's "preparatory work" took exactly forty years and ended in 1914. Was it not likely that a further period of forty years, commencing in 1914, would see "the end of all things"?[48]

In 1955 the Witnesses were told that "in the light of the fulfillment of Bible prophecy it is becoming clear that the war of Armageddon is nearing its breaking-out point."[49]

It was stated in 1963 that "it does no good to use Bible chronology for speculating on dates that are still future in the stream of time.—Matt. 24:36."[50] Yet the year 1966 saw just such speculation on the basis of viewing the 6,000 year chronology as running out in 1975.

---

[46] (Brooklyn: Watchtower Bible and Tract Society, 1950), p. 307.

[47] *Ibid.,* p. 311.

[48] *Jehovah's Witnesses and What They Believe* (Grand Rapids: Zondervan Publishing House, 1967), pp. 54, 55.

[49] *You May Survive Armageddon into God's New World* (Brooklyn: Watchtower Bible and Tract Society, 1955), p. 331.

[50] *All Scripture Is Inspired by God and Beneficial* (Brooklyn: Watchtower Bible and Tract Society, 1963), p. 286. See also the contrast between how Matthew 24:36 is viewed here and in *The Watchtower* issue of August 15, 1968, pp. 500, 501.

94   THE JEHOVAH'S WITNESSES AND PROPHETIC SPECULATION

What cataclysmic times are fast approaching! A climax in man's history is at the door! How vital, then, for each one who loves life to take note of these evidences of history that point to the near end of this wicked system![51]

In conclusion, a quotation from a 1969 *Watchtower,* typical of the statements down to the present, warns: "There is only a short time left before Jehovah will destroy this wicked system of things."[52] Armageddon could occur anytime now.

VII. CONCLUSION

It was the purpose of this chapter to show that the stress on the "last days" and the threat of Armageddon have been used first by Russell and Rutherford, and then by the Watchtower Society, to create an *illusion* of urgency. This illusion has kept the followers of the Society active and brought many new converts into the movement. The latest stress on 1975 has had its results in growth, for in 1970 there were 164,193 baptisms of new converts.[53] This number represents almost twice the number of baptisms just two years before when 82,842 were reported.[54] Even larger growth figures were recorded in the following years.

By way of conclusion, a chronological listing of statements excerpted from the quotations in this chapter is given. All of the pronouncements, except those with an asterisk (*), reflect the official Watchtower position at the time they were made.[55]

Year	Statement
1877	"THE END OF THIS WORLD . . . is nearer than most men suppose"
1886	"Marshalling of the hosts for the battle of the great day of

---

[51] *Awake!,* XLVII (October 8, 1966), p. 20.

[52] XC (January 15, 1969), p. 39.

[53] *The Watchtower,* XCII (January 1, 1971), p. 29.

[54] *The Watchtower,* XC (January 1, 1969), p. 25.

[55] Ellipses at the beginning and ending of the quotations are not employed.

POSITION ON "LAST DAYS" AND ARMAGEDDON

God Almighty, is in progress while the skirmishing is commencing"

1889 — "The 'battle of the great day of God Almighty' . . . which will end in A.D. 1914 . . . is already commenced"

1894 — "The skirmishing is already beginning all along the line" "The end of 1914 is not the date for the *beginning*, but for the *end* of the time of trouble"

1904 — "The stress of the great time of trouble will be on us soon, somewhere between 1910 and 1912–culminating . . . October 1914"

1914 — "The great crisis, the great clash . . . is very near" "Armageddon may begin next spring"

1915 — "The Battle of Armageddon, to which this war is leading"

1915? — "The present great war in Europe is the beginning of the Armageddon of the Scriptures"

1917 — "We anticipate that the 'earthquake' will occur early in 1918, and that the 'fire' will come in the fall of 1920"

1920 — Emphasis on 1925: "The old order of things, the old world, is ending" "We are standing at the very portals of that blessed time!" (Golden Age of the Kingdom) "Deliverance is at the door!"

1929 — "God's purpose now to shortly dash to pieces the Devil's organization" "Satan knows that shortly he must fight the Lord"

1930 — "The great climax is at hand"

1931 — "His day of vengeance is here, and Armageddon is at hand" "God's judgment . . . must shortly be executed"

1932* — The end was "only a short time away"

1939 — "The time for the battle of the great day of God Almighty is very near" "The disaster of Armageddon is just ahead"

1940 — "The day for final settlement is near at hand" "The witness work for THE THEOCRACY appears to be about done"

1941	"Armageddon is surely near ... soon ... within a few years"
1942	"THE NEW WORLD IS AT THE DOORS ... The time is short"
1943	"The beginning of the final war is dangerously near"
1944	"The end of the world arrangement is now near"
1946* (or before)	"Armageddon ... should come sometime before 1972"
1946	"The final end draws near"
1950	"Jehovah's time has come to settle definitely the issue"
1953*	"1954 could well be 'The Year!'"
1955	"The war of Armageddon is nearing its breakingout point"
1966	"A climax of man's history is at the door!"
1969	"There is only a short time left"

On the basis of past pronouncements, can the Watchtower Society be trusted as an accurate source of prophetic understanding?

APPENDIX
IS TIME RUNNING OUT FOR THE WITNESSES?
(Written in December 1975)

Since this book was first published in October 1972, this writer has followed with interest what has taken place among the Jehovah's Witnesses. Witness growth hit new peaks with 297,872 baptisms reported in 1974, and 295,073 in 1975. Certainly, the belief that 6,000 years of human history would end in 1975 and that Armageddon could also occur then (or sooner), spurred the Witnesses on to increased activity and brought thousands of new converts into the movement. How are these teachings concerning Bible chronology and Armageddon viewed at present? This Appendix surveys these subjects and gives observations on the latest developments.

THE SIGNIFICANCE OF 1975

On February 10, 1975, Society vice-president F. W. Franz addressed over 20,000 Witnesses in the Los Angeles Sports Arena. Thousands of others were linked by radio hookup to hear the message in other California locations. This was only one of a number of similar meetings held around the world to give the Society's latest information on the significance of 1975. It was obvious from what Mr. Franz said that the hopes for 1975 among many Witness were very high. "Faced with an anticipated Sept. 5 deadline and growing expectations among many Witnesses," observed John Dart, "F. W. Franz, the sect's 81-year-old chief 'theologian,' has put the damper on specific references to the war to end all wars." [1]

In his speech, "Time in Which We Are Now Interested," Franz stated that 6,000 years of human history would definitely end at sundown, September 5, 1975, according to the lunar calendar.[2] He also disclosed what many Witnesses around the world were expecting in 1975.

> Now [in] our inquiries around the world with brothers as to what they're expecting to occur between now and the end of 1975, it is revealed, that some, are very sanguine about matters in the near future, and they're expecting the great tribulation to occur and the destruction of Babylon the Great and the annihilation of all the political systems of this world and then the binding of Satan and his demons and their abyssing to occur before this year is ended. This year 1975. And immediately thereafter the thousand year reign of the Lord Jesus Christ to begin. So they expect a great deal. And they're venting their views to their brothers and sisters in the congregations and raising their expectations very, very high indeed. Well now, we're not saying that by the end of this year 1975 all these things cannot take place. That God

---

[1] John Dart, "The End is Near . . .Maybe," *Los Angeles Times*, February 24, 1975, Part 2, p. 1.

[2] F. W. Franz, Los Angeles Sports Arena, February 10, 1975 (tape recording). To announce that 6,000 years were certain to run out on September 5, 1975 would indicate that the problems of chronology mentioned in the August 15, 1968 *Watchtower* (pp. 499, 500) and in the article on "Abraham" in *Aid to Bible Understanding* (p. 23, where it is stated that an adjustment would place Adam's creation date as 4027 rather than 4026 B.C.E.) have been solved. The present writer is amazed at the Witnesses' certainty on such matters when the finest Bible scholars in the world have rejected the entire scheme of dating Adam's creation as being impossible on the basis of the available evidence.

cannot bring all these things about! He can! He's almighty. And this omnipotent One can bring this about in a hurry if He wants to do so. But, in view of what the Scriptures inform us, are we warranted in expecting so much to occur by September 5, 1975? . . .[3]

Franz went on to explain that there was a time interval between Adam's creation and Eve's, and that the sixth creative day ended only after Eve's creation. So while September 5, 1975, would mark the end of 6,000 years of man's existence, it did not mean that mankind would be 6,000 years into the seventh day. This view was also presented in the October 1, 1975 *Watchtower*. If this time interval were one month, then things could terminate in October, if two months, November, and so on. Franz stated, "Well, since that is the case, then we do not necessarily have to insist or even expect that everything is going to be through and over with by September 5 of this year. . . ."[4]

Reflecting the urgency which has characterized the movement for decades, Franz then cautioned his audience,

. . . After September 5, things could happen, and it looks very likely they're going to happen, according to the way that affairs are going in the world . . . .

. . . So it could come, quickly, within a short time after the terminal day of the lunar year 1975. And we should not jump to wrong decisions on that account and say, well, the time after September 5, 1975 is indefinitely long and so it will allow for me to realize my human aspirations, getting married and raising a family — kids; or, going to college for a few years and learning engineering and finding a fine position as an engineer . . . or some other prominent, fine paying job. No! The time does not allow for that dear friends . . . . Evidently there is not much time left . . . .[5]

So, according to current Watchtower speculation, Armageddon and the millennial reign of Christ could take place almost immediately — or at some time during the next few years.

SPECULATION ON 1975

In response to the question "What happened to previous

---

[3] F. W. Franz tape.

[4] *Ibid.*

[5] *Ibid.*

predictions concerning 1975?" the dedicated Witness today will usually deny that anything definite was predicted or believed. Witness Jim Heidt is quoted in the February 14, 1975 *Los Angeles Times* as saying that "it was only the immature brothers and sisters reading between the lines who felt that Armageddon was definitely predicted for 1975."[6] From the available evidence it would seem that a great number of Witnesses were "immature" and that these were the ones who contacted potential converts and talked with evangelical Christians. They also seemed to be the ones who were frequently quoted in the news media.

John Dart reported that "the Brooklyn-headquartered Watchtower Society, burned by past erroneous prophecies, maintains that it never has said flatly that 1975 was going to be IT," and then concluded, "But in fact the society has left its followers little else to conclude."[7] As with past "erroneous prophecies" The Witness leadership is placing blame for inflated hopes and speculation concerning 1975 on the average Jehovah's Witness. In addition to the statements by Heidt and Franz, the *Watchtower* of October 15, 1974, claimed that the publications of the Jehovah's Witnesses "have never said that the world's end would come then [1975]," and then added, "Nevertheless, there has been considerable individual speculation on the matter." What is not stated is that the source of the "individual speculation" was the Society and its publications.[8]

Contacts with Jehovah's Witnesses and those who have left the movement in the past few years verified the importance that they attached to 1975 and their expectation that Armageddon would take place that year or even before. On three occasions during 1974, in contacts from various parts of the United States (California, Nevada and Hawaii), it was learned from teachers and other sources that Witness parents were so sure Armageddon would come during 1975 at the latest, that they removed their children from school, giving this belief as the reason.

Recent conversations with Jehovah's Witnesses have been interesting. When one was asked what had happened to

---

[6] Dart, p. 5.

[7] *Ibid.*, p. 1.

[8] P. 635.

V   THE JEHOVAH'S WITNESSES AND PROPHETIC SPECULATION

Armageddon as previously predicted, the answer given was, "1975 is not over yet!" Another indicated that there was still almost a year available.

What did Witnesses believe and teach concerning 1975, according to newspaper reports? Here are a few representative articles. Under the headline, "Witnesses Give World Five Years at the Most," the Religion Editor of the *Arizona Republic* (August 24, 1969) presented an interview with Witness Erroll Burton.

> *Within months, or at the most five years, the end of the world as we have known it will occur* and a thousand-year reign of Jesus will begin [italics mine].
>
> This is the view of the approximately 400,000-member [in the USA] sect calling itself Jehovah's Witnesses.
>
> According to Erroll Burton, Paradise Valley Unit of Jehovah's Witnesses, the prediction is based on the estimate that 1975 will mark the end of 6,000 years since the time of Adam and Eve, and that according to scripture, is when Armageddon will occur (Rev. 16:16) . . . .

The March 19, 1970 issue of the English newspaper, *Daily Mail*, reported the story of how a Witness couple "refused permission for their newly born son to have a life-saving blood transfusion," but that their refusal was overturned by the magistrates at an emergency court hearing, and the transfusion was given. The parents held those responsible for the transfusion as "guilty of a grave sin." The article then went on to state: "The couple, who have been Witnesses for two years, believe that Armageddon—judgment day—will come before 1975. They said: 'If the baby died, he would have been resurrected and reunited with us after Armageddon.'" The *Evening Mail* of May 7, 1971, carried an article on the experiences of former Witnesses, Mr. and Mrs. Herman Goldvag who had left the movement in 1969. Mrs. Goldvag explained: "We want to prevent other people from going through the misery we have had. Missionaries are working hard in Birmingham to recruit more into the faith before 1975—the expected date of Armageddon."

"Witnesses Take the Plunge For Eternity" was the headline of the article which appeared in the July 25, 1973 *Los Angeles Times*. Reported Bella Stumbo covered the story of the baptismal service at the five-day Assembly at Dodger Stadium and interviewed some ladies waiting to be baptized:

But the plain fact is that doomsday is at hand, said Mrs. McGuire, 26, and those who haven't been baptized as Jehovah's Witnesses are going to perish.

The occasion, she elaborated, is called Armageddon and it is prophesied in the holy scriptures. By all the best Witness reckoning, its due in two to three years.

Rev. Frank Triggs of the Cerritos First Assembly of God Church reported that "the leader of a Jehovah's Witness congregation in Southern California was so convinced that Oct. 31, 1974, was the last possible date for Armageddon that he declared he would sell his home for a few dollars on Oct. 30."[9]

The following experience is taken from a written account by Eric Grieshaber and his wife Jean who resigned from the Jehovah's Witnesses on October 24, 1974.

As the time for Armageddon drew closer, "the friends" began selling their homes, campers and motorcycles. Many gave up good paying jobs and took janitorial work in order to have more time for service.

The year 1973 was an exciting one as we prepared for Armageddon. One of our friends who had left the area wrote and asked permission to stay with us in order to "ride out Armageddon" with the congregation. Two other families that moved to where the "need was greater" came back to our congregation to await Armageddon. We all knew that sometime around October 1, 1974 the last year of mankind's 6,000 years of existence on earth would begin and soon Jesus Christ would take his peaceful rule over the earth.

That many Witnesses did quit their jobs in anticipation of the soon advent of Armageddon is verified in the Witnesses' May 1974 issue of *Kingdom Ministry:*

Reports are heard of brothers selling their homes and property and planning to finish out the rest of their days in this old system in the pioneer service. Certainly this is a fine way to spend the short time remaining before the wicked world's end.

Another significant account dealing with Witness expectations for 1975 appeared in the January 1975 issue of the *Evangelical Times*, published in London. The article, "Will the World End This Year?" was written by Richard E. Cotton (in consultation with ex-Witness George Terry). Mr. Cotton had left the Witnesses after eighteen years. Only a portion of the article is reproduced here.

---

[9] Dart, p. 1.

THE JEHOVAH'S WITNESSES AND PROPHETIC SPECULATION

The year 1975 has dawned, and with it comes the question: Could this be the year of Nemesis, of retribution, for Jehovah's Witnesses? Could it be the year of yet another dashed hope?

To many of the rank and file within the Watchtower Movement, 1975 has meant only one thing — the long awaited year of Divine Wrath. The time of judgment, when God would destroy the wicked and restore this old earth to a paradise state. Eternal life in the restored earth has been the hope of most Jehovah's Witnesses.

For almost ten years 1975 has hung over the heads of the faithful like a chronological carrot. True, very little has been written about it in official Watchtower publications, but a great deal has been said at grassroot level. And when Witnesses are taught to believe that God is using the Watchtower organisation to the total exclusion of all other churches or bodies (for this is their claim) it only requires a hint of a date to begin a wave of speculation. This is very understandable in a group maintaining that we are living at the very end of the Bible's "time of the end".

A date like 1975 had a fine apocalyptic ring when it was still ten years or so ahead. In 1966 a publication called *Life Everlasting — in Freedom of the Sons of God* announced that independent research into Bible chronology had established that 6,000 years of human history would come to an end in the autumn of 1975. As Jehovah's Witnesses believe that there will be a millenium to complete a divine cycle of 7,000 years, it was clear that the long awaited period would begin around the autumn of 1975.

When the date was made public 1966, the present writer was a Witness and was able to see what happened. Very little apart from that statement was ever published, but things began to be said and great was the speculation. No doubt many can recall the famous football star who stated on television that the Bible taught that the end would come in 1975. He was so certain of this, viewers were told, that if the expected results did not materialise, he would throw his Bible away.

In the months and years that followed overseers and visiting speakers of the cult were known to speak to the congregation about the "short time left". Some of the more convinced would total up the number of days to October 1975. When told by indignant householders, "You people are always round at our doors," one full time worker would answer: "We shall not be calling many more times".

Bible Studies with the unconverted were limited to a certain number of weeks because of the nearness of the end. Some Witnesses never bothered to increase their mortgage repayments as interest rates shot upwards. They were hoping for a permanent settlement on the amount outstanding in 1975. Some were so convinced the world was on its last legs that they speculated the system could not last until 1975.

D.I.Y. fans in the movement were known to remark in the early '70s that the house would not need repainting ever again. There was even the

JW in need of surgery who preferred to live with the condition until the healing rays of the Millenium restored all to perfect health.

How many Witnesses, we wonder, will be suffering from loss of memory this year about their expressed hopes of only a year or so back? But these things were said and no amount of forgetting can unsay them.

To add to the fires of speculation some Witnesses got hold of typed copies of a talk which it was claimed was given by one of the Watchtower Directors in some far away country. This explosive material indicated that soon calamities and even flesh-consuming plagues of a cosmic nature would befall the world of men. Yet members of the Watchtower Movement would be untouched by these manifestations of divine anger.

How sure everyone seemed. Yet now 1975 is here and the dilemma of the Witnesses continues to increase . . . .

. . . .

But this is not all. Other problems now arise for the Witnesses' world view. They no longer have the luxury of being able to extend their time of waiting for still further years. For decades now the publications have emphasised that the second coming or presence of our Lord began in the year 1914. Using this year as a chronological anchor for the plan of the "last days", they confidently state ("from" Matt. 24:34) that in less than the passing of one human generation from 1914 all will be completed.

The honest observer may well be asking what many thinking JWs are asking. How long is a generation? From 1914 to 1975 is 61 years, a rather long time. If we think in terms of 40 years as a reasonable and scriptural figure then the cult has lost out. Even if we stretch the post - 1914 period to its full limit by giving it a full biblical "threescore years and ten", we still find problems.

As stated before, the Movement stresses that it is the generation that is alive and witnessed 1914 that will still be around when the final end comes. So we are dealing with a time period years less than a full 70 years.

Time is no longer on the side of the Watchtower. Their prophetic hourglass is empty, but for a few grains of sand.

As the critical year progresses, it may well be that pressure will be eased by diversionary tactics. We do not doubt the ability of the "men at the top" to make fresh calculations for the future, but the fact remains that this year may well be a critical one for the movement.[10]

---

[10] The *Evangelical Times* address is: *Evangelical Times*, Elephant and Castle, London, S.E.1.

THE ADAM AND EVE "GAP"

According to Watchtower publications and Witness vice-president F. W. Franz, the long-awaited Battle of Armageddon and the peaceful reign of Jesus Christ are delayed only by the time interval between Adam and Eve's creation. According to Witness materials, how long was this interval? Let us examine and compare Witness publications in answer to the question.

The *Watchtower* of October 1, 1975, in agreement with Mr. Franz's speech at the Sports Arena, stated: "It [the Bible] shows a time lapse between the creation of Adam and that of his wife, Eve. During that time, God had Adam name the animals. Whether that period amounted to weeks or months *or years* [italics mine], we do not know."[11] Compare this speculation, with what was stated in *The Watchtower* of August 15, 1968: "...After his creation Adam lived some time during the 'sixth day' ....And yet the end of that sixth creative 'day' could end within the same Gregorian calendar year of Adam's creation. It may involve only a difference of weeks or months, *not years*" [italics mine].[12] This second and earlier statement is in agreement with what had been published and stated by the Society leadership for years.

Was there anything else stated or published that would cause Witnesses to conclude that the end of the sixth creative day paralleled the beginning of the seventh day, or that the time interval was minimal, at the most less than a year? The answer is yes.

In the report on the "God's Sons of Liberty" District Assemblies, held in 1966, the *Watchtower* commented on the response to the release of the new book *Life Everlasting — in Freedom of the Sons of God*.

> Immediately its contents were examined. It did not take the brothers very long to find the chart beginning on page 31, showing that 6,000 years of man's existence end in 1975. Discussion of 1975 overshadowed about everything else. "The new book compels us to realize that

---

[11] P. 579.

[12] P. 499. Page 500 states: "So the lapse of time between Adam's creation and the end of the sixth creative day, though unknown, was a compartively short period of time."

Armageddon is, in fact, very close indeed," said one conventioner. Surely it was one of the outstanding blessings to be carried home! [13]

Why had 1975 become so important in 1966, when a chronology which agreed with it had already been published in 1963 in *All Scripture is Inspired of God and Beneficial?* Why had the 1963 publication not stirred the same response? Because this chronology was accompanied with the statement, "It does no good to use Bible chronology for speculating on dates that are still future in the stream of time."[14] The significance of the 1966 publication was that chronology *was* used for speculation on dates that are future in the stream of time. The stress in *Life Everlasting — in Freedom of the Sons of God* was that man's creation and the end of the sixth day were probably parallel to the beginning of the seventh. This book stated:

> According to this trustworthy Bible chronology six thousand years from man's creation will end in 1975, and the seventh period of a thousand years of human history will begin in the fall of 1975 C.E. . . .
>
> How appropriate it would be for Jehovah God to make of this coming seventh period of a thousand years a sabbath period of rest and release . . . . It would not be by mere chance or accident but would be according to the loving purpose of Jehovah God for the reign of Jesus Christ, the "Lord of the Sabbath," to run parallel with the seventh millennium of man's existence.[15]

It is obvious that in this statement there is no view of a time interval of years between Adam and Eve's creation. While the report on the Baltimore Assembly mentions that Mr. Franz cautioned the brethren, "Don't any of you be specific in saying anything that is going to happen between now and 1975," it was Mr. Franz himself, as the same report stated, who "went into some length showing the feasibility of the date 4026 B.C. as being the beginning of God's rest day."[16] (This is the same date assigned to Adam *and Eve's* creation.)

The new emphasis of the 1966 book on the year 1975 is clearly reiterated in the *Awake!* of October 8, 1966.

---

[13] October 15, 1966, pp. 628, 629.

[14] P. 286.

[15] Pp. 29, 30.

[16] *The Watchtower,* October 15, 1966, p. 631.

xi THE JEHOVAH'S WITNESSES AND PROPHETIC SPECULATION

> *Does God's rest day parallel the time man has been on earth since his creation? Apparently so.* From the most reliable investigations of Bible chronology, harmonizing with many accepted dates of secular history, we find that Adam was created in the autumn of the year 4026 B.C. Sometime in that same year Eve could well have been created, directly after which God's rest day commenced. *In what year, then, would the first 6,000 years of man's existence and also the first 6,000 years of God's rest day come to an end? The year 1975* [italics mine].[17]

The Watchtower of May 1, 1968, stated:

> .... It is logical that *he would create Eve soon after Adam, perhaps just a few weeks or months later in the same year, 4026 B.C.E.* After her creation, God's rest day, the seventh period, immediately followed.
>
> *Therefore, God's seventh day and the time man has been on earth apparently run parallel.* To calculate where man is in the stream of time relative to God's seventh day of 7,000 years, we need to determine how long a time has elapsed from *the year of Adam and Eve's creation in 4026 B.C.E.* . . . Thus, eight years remain to account for a full 6,000 years of the seventh day. *Eight years from the autumn of 1967 would bring us to the autumn of 1975, fully 6,000 years into God's seventh day, his rest day* [italics mine].[18]

The *Awake!* of October 8, 1968 stated that "according to reliable Bible chronology, *Adam and Eve* [italics mine] were created in 4026 B.C."[19]

The Jehovah's Witnesses continued to teach that Adam and Eve were both created in the calendar year 4026 B.C.E. and that the seventh day commenced in that same year. For example, Genesis 5:3 states that "Adam lived on for a hundred and thirty years. Then he became father to a son in his likeness, in his image, and called his name Seth" (NWT). In the article on "Eve" in *Aid to Bible Understanding*, the reader is told: "At the age of 130 another son was born to her. Eve called his name Seth. . . ."[20] Certainly if Adam and Eve were *both* 130 years of age at Seth's birth, the time gap between their creation could not have been lengthy. And finally, in the 1974 publication, *God's "Eternal Purpose" Now Triumphing for Man's Good*, there is a

---

[17] P. 19.

[18] P. 271.

[19] P. 14.

[20] (Brooklyn: Watchtower Bible and Tract Society, 1969), p. 538.

bold heading which states, "'EVENING' OF SEVENTH CREATIVE 'DAY' BEGINS, 4026 B.C.E."[21] If this date was just speculation, or a guess, it should not have been used as a major division of the book.

In conclusion, it is obvious that if one takes Witness statements and publications seriously—although there have been attempts recently to gain years of time — they have limited the time available before Armageddon occurs to less than a year.

ARE THE GENESIS DAYS 7,000 YEARS LONG?

In agreement with C. T. Russell the Witnesses teach that the Genesis "days" are 7,000-year periods, not 24-hour days. If it could be shown that these days were not 7,000 years long, but days of approximately 24 hours, the current Witness speculation as to the time interval between Adam and Eve's creation would no longer be available, for both would have been created during one solar day.

It is not this writer's intention to give a lengthy development of this point here. It is true as Dr. Raymond Surburg stated after examining several views,

> Despite these many variant ideas concerning the meaning of *yom* [day], there is an impressive amount of evidence favoring the view that the "days" referred to in connection with the creative activity of God were not long periods but solar days of approximately 24 hours.[22] [For a brief presentation of some of the evidence mentioned by Surburg, see Appendix E.]

CONCLUSION

This Appendix asks the question, "Is time running out for the Witnesses?" The answer is yes. Or more accurately, it could be said that time has already run out. It is also obvious that the speculation which has characterized the history of this movement since its inception still continues.

When in his Sports Arena address, F. W. Franz cautioned his audience not to come to wrong conclusions concerning the time

---

[21] P. 51.

[22] "In the Beginning God Created," Chapter 2 of *Darwin, Evolution and Creation* (St. Louis: Concordia Publishing House, 1959, p. 59.

available — to realize their human aspirations of marriage, family, education and job — he reminded this writer of the similar instructions that were given by the Witness leadership during World War II. For example, in the summer of 1941, J. F. Rutherford questioned the wisdom of marrying because of the closeness of Armageddon and the Millennial Kingdom. He asked, " 'Why, then, should a man who has the prospect before him of being of the great multitude now tie himself up to a stack of bones and a hank of hair?' "[23] This statement agreed with the book *Children* which was also released in 1941.[24] How close was Armageddon according to the *Watchtower* magazine of September 15, 1941? It was reported that the book *Children* (distributed to children at the St. Louis convention) was "the Lord's provided instrument for most effective work in the *remaining months before Armageddon* [italics mine]."[25] Certainly the piper's tune has not changed!

---

[23] *The Watchtower*, September 15, 1941, p. 287.

[24] See p. 366.

[25] P. 288.

CHAPTER 6

FALSE ADVERTISING, FALSE PROPHECY AND FALSE CHRISTIANITY

In this chapter it will be shown that the Watchtower Society is guilty of false advertising, that it stands condemned by its own words as a false prophet and that it requires its faithful membership to accept unreservedly its pronouncements under the threat of disfellowshiping and ultimate annihilation.

I. FALSE ADVERTISING

After the reader has studied the book to this point he cannot help but be aware of the fact that *The Watchtower* has taken its readers through a maze of conflicting and contradictory interpretations. Statements have been quoted from this magazine which are irreconcilable. Yet, in spite of this glaring lack of consistency, actually *undependability,* the following was published in advertising *The Watchtower:*

> Since 1879 it has been published regularly for the benefit of sincere students of the Bible. Over that extended period of time *The Watchtower* has consistently proven itself dependable.[1]

How could a claim be more blatantly false? Jehovah's Witnesses who today would accept and propagate the prophetic understanding and time calculations of earlier Watchtower positions would actually be disfellowshiped!

Another example of false advertising relative to *The Watchtower* is found on the back cover of the January 8, 1970 issue of *Awake!*

---

[1] *New World Translation of the Christian Greek Scriptures* (Brooklyn: Watchtower Bible and Tract Society, 1950), p. 793.

For ninety years this faithful journal has been pointing forward to this very time, urging people to turn to the Bible because of the spiritual famine that the Bible itself foretold was to come in our generation.

It is obvious from what has been presented elsewhere in this book, that this statement is also false and that it almost completely expunges the prophetic interpretations, observations and views on chronology given by Russell between 1877 and 1914. The present Witness leadership has cleverly and conveniently forgotten the past!

The fact remains that these two ads for *The Watchtower* are obvious examples of *false advertising.*

II. FALSE PROPHECY

It is one thing for the present writer, on the basis of the Bible and other evidence, to declare that the Watchtower Society is guilty of false prophecy and that individuals such as Russell, Rutherford and other leaders were individually false prophets. It is another thing to find that the Society, through its own publications, reveals itself and its leaders to be false prophets without God's enlightenment. How can this be?

The following is quoted from the October 8, 1968 *Awake!* article, "A Time to 'Lift Up Your Head' in Confident Hope":

> True, there have been those in times past who predicted an "end to the world," even announcing a specific date. Some have gathered groups of people with them and fled to the hills or withdrawn into their homes waiting for the end. Yet, nothing happened. The "end" did not come. They were guilty of false prophesying. Why? What was missing?
>
> Missing was the full measure of evidence required in fulfillment of Bible prophecy. Missing from such people were God's truths and the evidence that he was guiding and using them.[2]

While it is true that the Bible Students or Witnesses of today did not flee to the hills or withdraw to their homes to wait for the end, it is also true that the movement did set specific dates for the "end of the world," for example, 1914. Such an erroneous prediction would make them, too, "guilty of false prophesying." How is this false prophesying explained? "Missing from

---

[2] XLIX (October 8, 1968), p. 23.

such people were God's truths and the evidence that he was guiding and using them" says *Awake!* Would this not also apply to the Watchtower Society? Surely the Society cannot escape the implications of its own words.[3]

III. FALSE PROPHECY AND FALSE CHRISTIANITY

That false prophecy and wrong dates for events of the "last days" have been published by the Society has already been established. What makes these errors even more reprehensible is that Jehovah's Witnesses must accept them as they are published, without questioning. The Society may change its views on an interpretation at any time. But a Witness who, after the study of the Watchtower understanding of a passage, concluded that it was wrong and persisted in this view *before* it was so identified by the Society, would be disfellowshiped. It is clear from the portion of the trial transcript which follows, that the authority of the Watchtower hierarchy, and the unity of the organization shown by support of the Witnesses' current views are *more important than truth* to the Society's leadership. The testimony is taken from the Pursuer's Proof of a trial held in the Scottish Court of Sessions, in November, 1954. Legal counsel for the Society, Haydon C. Covington, answered the questions of the attorney for the Ministry of Labour and National Service.

Q. You have promulgated—forgive the word—false prophecy:
A. We have—I do not think we have promulgated false prophecy, there have been statements that were erroneous, that is the way I put it, and mistaken.
Q. ... It was promulgated as a matter which must be believed by all members of Jehovah's Witnesses that the Lord's Second Coming took place in 1874?
A. I am not familiar with that. You are speaking on a matter that I know nothing of....
Q. You have studied the literature of your movement?
A. Yes, but not all of it. I have not studied the seven volumes of "Studies in the Scriptures," and I have not studied this matter that you are mentioning now of 1874. I am not at all familiar with that.
Q. Assume from me that it was promulgated as authoritative by the Society that Christ's Second Coming was in 1874?

---

[3] *Ibid.*

A. Taking that assumption as a fact, it is a hypothetical statement.
Q. That was the publication of false prophecy?
A. That was the publication of a false prophecy, it was a false statement or an erroneous statement in fulfilment of a prophecy that was false or erroneous.
Q. And that had to be believed by the whole of Jehovah's Witnesses?
A. Yes, because you must understand we must have unity, we cannot have disunity with a lot of people going every way, an army is supposed to march in step....
Q. Back to the point now. A false prophecy was promulgated?
A. I agree to that.
Q. It had to be accepted by Jehovah's Witnesses?
A. That is correct.
Q. If a member of Jehovah's Witnesses took the view himself that that prophecy was wrong and said so he would be disfellowshiped?
A. Yes, if he said so and kept persisting in creating trouble, because if the whole organisation believes one thing, even though it be erroneous and somebody else starts on his own trying to put his ideas across then there is disunity and trouble, there cannot be harmony, there cannot be marching together. When a change comes it should come from the proper source, the head of the organisation, the governing body, not from the bottom upwards, because everybody would have ideas, and the organisation would disintegrate and go in a thousand different directions. Our purpose is to have unity.
Q. Unity at all costs?
A. Unity at all costs, because we believe and are sure that Jehovah God is using our organisation, the governing body of our organisation to direct it, even though mistakes are made from time to time.
Q. And unity based upon an enforced acceptance of false prophecy?
A. That is conceded to be true.
Q. And the person who expressed his view, as you say, that it was wrong, and was disfellowshiped, would be in breach of the Covenant, if he was baptized?
A. That is correct.
Q. And as you said yesterday expressly, would be worthy of death?
A. I think –
Q. Would you say yes or no?
A. I will answer yes, unhesitatingly.
Q. Do you call that religion?
A. It certainly is.
Q. Do you call it Christianity?
A. I certainly do.[4]

---

[4] A microfilm copy of the complete trial can be obtained from: The Scottish Record Office, H. M. General Register House, Edinburgh, Scotland. The order should

Covington's testimony for the Society is certainly significant. (1) As the Society's legal counsel and its former Vice-president, he admits that he had never even read the seven volumes of *Studies in the Scriptures,* all of which, except for the last volume, were written by C. T. Russell, the Society's founder! (2) He agrees that the Society had been guilty of publishing and promulgating "false prophecy." (3) The statements he makes or accepts concerning unity are certainly an example of false, not true Christianity. A "unity at all costs . . . based upon an enforced acceptance of false prophecy" under the penalty of eternal death, is not Christian teaching. It is not surprising that the attorney asked Covington: "Do you call it Christianity?" A true Christian unity is not created, sustained, safeguarded and enforced by any human institution. Where in the Bible does one find the principle or statement that God urges "unity at all costs" or at the expense of the truth? Such a position as that set forth by Covington as the representative of the Watchtower Society must be rejected as a clear example of *false Christianity.*

---

ask for the Pursuer's Proof of Douglas Walsh vs. The Right Honourable James Latham Clyde, M.P., P.C., as representing the Minister of Labour and National Service. The microfilm copy costs a little over $35.00. The pages quoted above were pp. 340-343. Obvious errors of *spelling* have been corrected without so indicating in the quote.

Chapter 7

CONCLUSIONS AND A PERSONAL TESTIMONY

A review of some of the important conclusions reached in this study are now to be stated. The important question, "Why a Witness of Jesus Christ—Not a Jehovah's Witness?"—which relates to the author's own experiences, concludes the chapter.

I. CONCLUSIONS

In the Introduction to this work the crucial importance of 1914 to the Witnesses was reviewed. It was pointed out that if this date was incorrect,

> not only would the claim that the Society represents God's visible organization and "channel" for the revelation of His truth for this age be invalidated, but the major teachings in a number of Witness books and magazines must, of necessity, be rejected . . . .

The Witnesses' position on 1914 was first stated, then it was examined and found to be incorrect. Thus, the Introduction's statements must be applied. The Society does not represent God's visible organization and "channel." On this point alone, many of its major teachings must be rejected.

The methods employed in the calculation of 1975 were examined and found to be unsound. Many problems inherent in the Witnesses' 6,000-year theory would indicate that the approach, as well as the view itself, is untenable. In addition, 1975 is now past history.

The survey in Chapter 5 of the pronouncements by the Society since its beginning, should convince any objective researcher that this movement stands guilty of false prophecy. It should also convince him that urgency and the stress on Armageddon have been utilized by the Society to gain converts and to stimulate the Witnesses to greater activity. As Chapter 6 showed, the Watchtower Society has even distorted its own history and the Bible in order to better exploit its eschatological emphasis and hierarchical authority.

From all that has been presented, the Watchtower Bible and Tract Society's claim, "that 'THE SOCIETY' is the visible representative of the Lord on earth" and "under the direct supervision of Christ Jesus at the Temple,"[1] rests on the slender thread of its own identification, a self-identification which is impossible to maintain in the light of the present study.

II. WHY A WITNESS OF JESUS CHRIST—NOT A JEHOVAH'S WITNESS?

Shortly after this writer had been "born again" (I John 5:1-5; John 3:3-7) by the simple acceptance of what the Bible stated, he encountered a new emphasis in his contacts with true Christians. This new emphasis was the prominence given to the name of the Lord Jesus Christ, in contrast to that of Jehovah so often stressed by the Jehovah's Witnesses. The question which confronted this writer was, "Which position was right—Why the emphasis on Jesus Christ?"

The answer was found in the New Testament. The message preached by the Christian believers during the first century is recorded in the Book of Acts—the church carrying forth the commission received from Christ (Matt. 28:18-20; Acts 1:8). Without exception, the salvation message of the early church centered on the theme of the Person and Work of Jesus Christ, His death and resurrection.[2] The Bible witnesses were witnesses of Jesus Christ! The Saviour spoke to His own before His ascension and said:

> But YOU will receive power when the holy spirit arrives upon YOU, and YOU will be witnesses of me both in Jerusalem and in all Judea and Samaria and to the most distant part of the earth. (Acts 1:8, *New World Translation*)

---

[1] *The Watchtower*, 1938, p. 182, cited in *The Watchtower*, LXXVI (June 1, 1955), p. 333.

[2] For the message of the early church in Acts: 2:22-40; 3:13-26; 4:2, 10-12, 33; 5:30-32, 42; 8:4-6, 35; 9:20; 10:39-43; 11:20, 26; 13:28-41; 16:30-32; 17:2-4, 18, 31; 18:5; 19:13; 20:21; 24:24; 26:22, 23.

"You will be witnesses of me," reveals that the message of the early church was to be the simple message of who Jesus Christ was and what He had done. A further study of Acts shows that except for quotations from the Old Testament, the name in which the work of the ministry was carried forth was the name of Jesus Christ.[3] Richard B. Rackham wrote:

> To the Jews the revelation of God was summed up in *the Name*, i.e., the divine name of JHVH which might not be uttered; but in the Acts the *Name* is always that of Jesus Christ; the Christians *call upon His name* (as upon that of JHVH), and his name is borne by them.[4]

In further explanation Rackham stated:

> The Israel of old had been separated from the world by the Name of JEHOVAH. They were the people who called upon the Name of the Lord and upon whom his Name was called. But the divine Name which the new sect bears is *the Name* of the Lord Jesus Christ. Into this Name they were baptized; in it they live and speak and work; for it they suffer. Accordingly by "this Name" they are known. They are the people "who call upon the name of the Lord Jesus"; and "upon whom his name is called." And when at last a distinctive name had to be invented for the new body, it was taken from this Name, and they were called CHRISTIANS. The Jews however could not recognize a name which implied the truth of this faith . . . . So they called his disciples in contempt Nazarenes or Galileans.[5]

To follow in the footsteps of the Christian witnesses of the Bible, then, an individual or a group must be a witness of Jesus Christ—a witness of His sacrificial death, His burial and glorious resurrection. Through this message alone it is proclaimed that "there is no salvation in anyone else, for there is not another name under heaven that has been given among men by which we must get saved" (Acts 4:12, *New World Translation*).

Those who rejected the testimony of Jesus Christ during His earthly ministry would not place themselves under the only name of salvation in Acts 4:12 and the commission of Acts 1:8 and "remained Jehovah's Witnesses."[6]

---

[3] Acts 2:38; 3:6, 16; 4:7, 10, 12, 17, 18, 30; 5:28, 40, 41; 8:12, 16; 9:14-16, 21, 27, 29; 10:43, 48; 15:26; 16:18; 19:5, 13, 17; 21:13; 22:16.

[4] *The Acts of the Apostles* (fourteenth ed.; London: Methuen and Co., Ltd., 1901), p. lxxiii.

[5] *Ibid.*, p. 76.

[6] Philip Elliot, *"Jehovah's Witnesses" in the First and Twentieth Centuries* (Second ed. revised; Stirling, Scotland: Drummond Tract Dept, n.d.), p. 15.

In his booklet, *"Jehovah's Witnesses" in the First and Twentieth Centuries,* Philip Elliott presented parallels between the Jehovah's witnesses (Israel, Isa. 43:10, 11) of Jesus' day and the modern Jehovah's Witnesses. The twentieth century Jehovah's Witnesses are in the same position of unbelief as the rejecting Jews of the New Testament: they deny the Deity and bodily resurrection of Christ, and they oppose the church of Christ. In so doing they reject the work of the Holy Spirit within every believer. Elliott concluded: "They are just as much in the dark as were the Jehovah's Witnesses of the first century."[7]

Walter E. Stuermann also saw the strong Old Testament Judaistic emphasis of the group and observed:

> Almost everywhere they subordinate Christian and New Testament themes to those of Judaism and the Old Testament. One wonders sometimes whether Jehovah might not just as well dispense with his chief executive officer, Jesus Christ. They will, of course, vigorously deny it; but, in this writer's judgment, the Witnesses are more accurately considered a mutation of a conservative, apocalyptic Judaism rather than a variant of Christianity.[8]

That Stuermann was right is illustrated by a former Jehovah's Witness who wrote to *Christianity Today:*

> I was raised a Baptist, but in my teen years became associated with Jehovah's Witnesses. While I maintain great respect for their fundamental knowledge of Bible *texts* and morality, my six years with them left me in a spiritual dearth. Why? No Christ! How wonderful it is to read and hear about Christ again! One learns a lot about ancient Israelitish history from them, but so little about Christ.[9]

In addition to the references already cited, the name of Jesus Christ as the object of faith permeates the Bible. Those who are saved, or are to receive salvation, must "believe in his name" (John 1:12; 2:23; 3:18; I John 5:13; 3:23). Christians are baptized in the name of Christ (Acts 2:38; 8:16; 10:48; 19:4, 5). Christians suffer in the name or for the name of Christ (Acts 5:41; 15:26; 21:13). Christians are to gather together in the name of Jesus Christ (Matt. 18:20; I Cor. 5:4). Every creature

---

[7] *Ibid.,* pp. 16-22.

[8] "The Bible and Modern Religions: III. Jehovah's Witnesses," *Interpretation,* X (July 1956), p. 345.

[9] IX (December 18, 1964), p. 305.

will render homage to Jesus Christ: "... At the name of Jesus Christ every knee should bow..." (Phil. 2:10). The instruction is given to "do all in the name of the Lord Jesus..." (Col. 3:17). Finally, it is in the name of Jesus that Christians have been cleansed, sanctified and justified (I Cor. 6:11).

Every true Christian has confessed "that Jesus Christ is Lord" (Phil. 2:11). The requirements for salvation are clearly stated by Paul in Romans 10:9: "That if thou shalt confess with thy mouth the Lord Jesus, and shalt believe in thine heart that God hath raised him from the dead, thou shalt be saved."

At the beginning of this study the writer stated that he had been "born again." He also can give witness to the knowledge that he has everlasting life. On what basis? On the basis of God's Word, accepted and believed without sectarian tradition or organizational "progressive light." Two questions should be considered. "Who are born again?" "Can one know that he has everlasting life?" The answers to these questions will be brief.

Quoting from I John 5:1-5 in the *New World Translation:*

> Everyone believing that Jesus is the Christ has been born from God, and everyone who loves the one that caused to be born loves him who has been born from that one. By this we gain the knowledge that we are loving the children of God, when we are loving God and doing his commandments. For this is what the love of God means, that we observe his commandments; and yet his commandments are not burdensome, because everything that has been born from God conquers the world. And this is the conquest that has conquered the world, our faith.
>
> Who is the one that conquers the world but he who has faith that Jesus is the Son of God?

Can the reader answer "yes" to the following two questions? (1) "Do I believe that Jesus is the Christ?" (2) "Do I believe that Jesus is the Son of God?" If the answers are "yes," he must accept the testimony that he must also be "born from God." It is an arbitrary interpretation which would steal the "born again" experience from all who would become Christians. Yet, the Watchtower Society has taken these verses and others away from the average Witness who is said to be a member of the "Great Multitude."[10]

---

[10] It was in 1935 that Joseph F. Rutherford presented a new interpretation which took away being Spirit begotten and the heavenly hope from the "Great Multitude" ("Great Company" or "Great Crowd"). Until this time it was taught that

Another passage should be examined. John 3:3-7 mentions the "born again" experience several times. Verse 3 in the *New World Translation* reads in part, "Most truly I say to you, Unless anyone is born again, he cannot see the kingdom of God." Verse 5 would indicate that to "see" the kingdom of God means to enter into it. The Witnesses claim that only the heavenly class (144,000) can make up or enter the kingdom.[11] The faithful men of old, such as Abel, Abraham, Isaac, and Jacob and the prophets, according to the Witnesses, are not in the kingdom of God but will be representatives of God on the earth and subjects under the kingdom.[12] This position is not in accord with what Scripture demands in Luke 13:28, 29:

> ... When YOU see Abraham and Isaac and Jacob and all the prophets in the kingdom of God, but yourselves thrown outside. Furthermore, people will come from eastern parts and western, and from the north and south, and will recline at the table in the kingdom of God.

Matthew 8:11, 12 is a parallel passage which substitutes "kingdom of the heavens" for "kingdom of God." Acceptance

---

this class was made up of "second-rate spirit begotten Christians." (For a full development of thinking relative to the "Great Multitude" see: *The Watchtower*, February 15, 1966 issue, pp. 116-123).

Russell's teaching is clear in the question and answer in *What Pastor Russell Said*. "*Question (1909)–1–Does the Great Company receive life direct from God on the spirit plane?* Answer—Yes, they receive life direct in that they have been begotten of the Holy Spirit, and when they are begotten they are just the same way as the little flock, because we are called in the one hope of our calling. They do not make their calling and election sure, but not being worthy of second death, they therefore receive life on the spirit plane" (p. 297).

In 1932 Rutherford stated: "Ever and anon someone advances the conclusion that the 'great multitude' will not be a spiritual class. The prophecy of Ezekiel shows that such conclusion is erroneous. The fact that their position is seven steps higher than the outside shows that they must be made spirit creatures ... They must be spirit creatures in order to be in the outer court of the divine structure, described by Ezekiel" (*Vindication*, III, p. 204).

Rutherford's statement that the "great multitude" members "must be spirit creatures" has the ring of certainty! And why not? In the introduction of the same volume one reads: "That vision of Ezekiel concerning the temple has been a mystery for ages and generations, but now is due to be understood. The Scriptures and the physical facts both show that this prophecy was not due to be understood by God's people on earth until the year 1932" (p. 5). This "due to be understood" position on the "Great Multitude" was rejected in 1935! Can Rutherford's interpretations be accepted as from God?

A question for the reader: "Where in the Bible does it say that only the 144,000 will be Spirit begotten or 'born again'?"

[11] *Let God Be True* (second ed.; Brooklyn: Watchtower Bible and Tract Society, 1946), pp. 136-138.

[12] *Ibid.*, p. 263.

of these two passages refutes the Witnesses' understanding of who are to be "in" the kingdom of God. So when Jesus said "YOU people must be born again" (John 3:7), for entrance into the kingdom of God, it meant that *all* must be "born again," without exception!

Can one know that he has everlasting life? The reader is referred to the *New World Translation* at I John 5:9-13.

> If we receive the witnesses men give, the witness God gives is greater, because this is the witness God gives, the fact that he has borne witness concerning his Son. The [person] putting his faith in the Son of God has the witness given, in his own case. The [person] not having faith in God has made him a liar, because he has not put his faith in the witness given, which God as witness has given concerning his Son. And this is the witness given, that God gave us everlasting life, and this life is in his Son. He that has the Son has this life; he that does not have the Son of God does not have this life.
>
> I write YOU these things that YOU may know that YOU have life everlasting, YOU who put YOUR faith in the name of the Son of God.

Each honest person who wishes to please God is urged to examine what is stated in the above passage. Let the reader answer the following questions directly from the Bible without recourse to outside interpretations. (1) How does one make God a liar? (2) What is the witness concerning Jesus Christ? (3) How does one receive everlasting life? (4) Can one know that he has (right now) life everlasting? (5) Do you accept God's witness?

Do you accept the testimony of Jesus Christ in John 6:47? "Most truly I say to YOU, he that believes has everlasting life." (*NWT*)[13]

Can the reader say, "I have been 'born again.' I know that I have life everlasting?" God can give that assurance![14]

A final word. Although it was never indicated in the book elsewhere, the author deeply believes that the return of Christ is very near. He also accepts the words of the Lord in Matthew

---

[13] Read John 6:35–65, especially verses 35 and 40.

[14] This section, "Why a Witness of Jesus Christ–Not a Jehovah's Witness?" is available in tract form at $4.50 per hundred postpaid. Further information on this and other subjects are found in the author's 332-page book, *Apostles of Denial: An Examination and Expose of the History, Doctrines and Claims of the Jehovah's Witnesses*, published by Presbyterian and Reformed Publishing Company (1970). The book ($8.95 postpaid) and the tract may be obtained from: Department of Apologetics, The Master's College, Newhall, California 91322.

24:36 where He said "of that day and hour knoweth no man." Christ's Second Coming is the "blessed hope" of all Christians (Titus 2:13). The way to be ready for His coming is not by date setting or by joining an organization, especially one which urges membership with the words: "Therefore, take steps quickly to work for survival and for eternal life in God's new order."[15]

Salvation is not offered by God on the basis of human work or effort, but on the basis of: (1) a recognition that one is a sinner (Rom. 3:23), (2) a recognition that Christ died to meet the sinner's need (John 3:16) and (3) repentance from sin and belief in Christ (Acts 17:30; Acts 16:31; John 1:12, 13). True salvation, grounded in God's grace and received by faith as God's gift will *result* in "good works" (Eph. 2:8-10).

A person who truly knows Christ as Saviour and Lord can begin and end each day with the words recorded in Revelation 22:20, "Even so, come Lord Jesus."

---

[15] *Awake!* XLIX (October 8, 1968), p. 29.

APPENDIX A

THE GREAT PYRAMID OF EGYPT

With the publication in 1859 of the book, *The Great Pyramid: Why Was It Built? And Who Built It?* by John Taylor, "modern Pyramidology was born."[1] Taylor was convinced that the Great Pyramid of Cheops at Gizeh was constructed by an Israelite architect working under divine direction. Taylor and others who accepted the theory put forward a number of Bible passages which they accepted as referring to this Pyramid (Isa. 19:19-20; Job 38:5-7; Eph. 2:20-21).[2] The Pyramid was viewed as

> divinely intended to prophetically reveal a mass of chronological data, a vast stone structure that would, when properly understood, indicate the years, and sometimes the months and very days of the major events in the redemptive program of the world.[3]

The theory was given prestige when the Astronomer-Royal of Scotland and Professor of Astronomy at Edinburgh, Charles Piazzi Smyth, made a personal study of Taylor's theory. Smyth's 664-page book, *Our Inheritance in the Great Pyramid*, first published in 1864, became the foundation of modern Pyramidology. In 1865 Smyth made a trip to Egypt to make his own measurements of the Pyramid and the results of his study were published in the three-volume *Life, and Work at the Great*

---

[1] Martin Gardner, *Fads and Fallacies in the Name of Science* (revised ed.; New York: Dover Publications, Inc., 1957), p. 174.

[2] *Ibid.*, p. 175. Russell began his chapter on the Pyramid in *Thy Kingdom Come* (p. 313) with the quotation of Isaiah 19:19-20. The other references cited above were also quoted in the chapter along with many other passages.

[3] Wilbur M. Smith, *Egypt in Biblical Prophecy* (Boston: W. A. Wilde Company, 1957), p. 210.

Pyramid (1867) and *On the Antiquity of Intellectual Man* (1868).[4]

C. T. Russell was impressed with Smyth's work and when the third volume of *Studies in the Scriptures (Thy Kingdom Come)* was published in 1891, an entire chapter of more than sixty pages was devoted to the Pyramid. The chapter entitled "The Testimony of God's Stone Witness and Prophet, the Great Pyramid in Egypt," is prefaced by a letter from Professor Smyth commending Russell's treatment of the Pyramid (p. 312).

Russell actually made two trips to visit the Great Pyramid; his first was in 1892 and his second, in 1910. Concerning his second visit Russell reported: "We merely reviewed this Great Witness to the Lord of hosts and recalled to mind its testimony . . . ."[5]

Russell's work on the Pyramid caused two brothers in England, John and Morton Edgar, to go to Egypt and there they also made first-hand measurements of their own. Two books resulted from their work: the first was published in 1910 and the second in 1913, under the title of *The Great Pyramid Passages and Chambers.* Both of these volumes were advertized in the *Watch Tower.*[6]

The Pyramid is discussed in a short article in the March 15, 1911 *Watch Tower,* which concludes:

> No doubt all of our readers have read STUDIES IN THE SCRIPTURES, Vol. III, the last chapter of which describes the Pyramid and sets forth much of the wonderful symbolic teachings shown in its construction. It shows the Pyramid to be in exact harmony with the Bible. Indeed, some, after reading this volume, have referred to the Great Pyramid as "The Bible in Stone."[7]

The great Pyramid was said to support the 1874, 1878, 1881 and 1914 dates Russell had determined by the Bible. Concerning this last date, Russell and "many of the dear friends" were

---

[4] Gardner, p. 176.

[5] *Watch Tower Reprints,* V (June 1, 1910), p. 4621.

[6] Gardner, p. 181. *Watch Tower Reprints,* V (August 1, 1910), p. 4658; VI (October 15, 1913), p. 5336. Rogerson mentions a third *Great Pyramid Passages* volume in *Millions Now Living Will Never Die*, p. 197, note 28.

[7] *Watch Tower Reprints,* V, p. 4790.

rejoicing over the seven corroborative proofs set forth in Morton Edgar's book which showed "that the close of the year 1914 ... will mark the closing of the Times of the Gentiles, and the beginning of the Messianic reign."[8]

It is worthy of note that the statements and measurements in *Thy Kingdom Come* were altered. (Compare the two editions below; later edition changes are in brackets.)

> Then measuring *down* the "Entrance Passage" from that point, to find the distance to the entrance of the "Pit," representing the great trouble and destruction with which this age is to close, when evil will be overthrown from power, we find it to be 3416 [3457] inches, symbolizing 3416 [3457] years from the above date, B.C. 1542. This calculation shows A.D. 1874 [1915] as marking the beginning of the period of trouble; for 1542 years B.C. plus 1874 [1915] years A.D. equals 3416 [3457]. Thus the Pyramid witness that the close of 1874 [1914] was the *chronological* beginning of the time of trouble ... [that the close of 1914 will be the beginning].[9]

Although alterations were made later, the smaller figures were defended by Russell as accurate in 1904: "We have no reason to question the accuracy of the figures given in Dawn III [early edition]." "We cannot therefore see how any *longer* measure for the passage could be possible."[10] Yet, the edition of 1907 had already been changed to the larger figures.

The teachings concerning the Great Pyramid were discarded by J. F. Rutherford, Russell's successor, about twelve years after his death.

> Writing in the November 15 and December 1, 1928, issues of *The Watch Tower and Herald,* Rutherford releases a double-barreled blast against it, and advances many ingenious arguments that the so-called Altar in Egypt was really inspired by Satan for the purpose of misleading the faithful. Did Jesus ever mention the Pyramid? Of course not. To study it, the Judge writes, is a waste of time and indicates lack of faith in the all-sufficiency of the Bible.[11]

---

[8] *Watch Tower Reprints,* VI (October 15, 1913), p. 5336.

[9] Russell, p. 342. Figure and word changes in brackets are found in the 1907 edition. For other changes compare pages 362-364 in the original and later editions (such as 1924).

In the edition of *Thy Kingdom Come* published by the Laymen's Home Missionary Movement and edited by Paul S. L. Johnson the pyramid measurements of Edgar are noted in brackets. Instead of either the 3416 of the earlier edition or the 3457 of the later editions, the Edgar figure is 3388.5!

[10] *Watch Tower Reprints,* IV (November 1, 1904), p. 3451.

[11] Gardner, p. 182.

APPENDIX A: THE GREAT PYRAMID OF EGYPT 113

The acceptance of Pyramidology by Russell, and for a time after his death by the Society, is of some significance. As a previous chapter pointed out, advertising for *The Watchtower* stated that since its inception in 1879 it "has consistently proven itself dependable."[12] A number of issues of this "dependable" magazine supported Pyramidology and some advertised and sold works on the subject. This is even more shocking when it is realized that "the Great Pyramid of Egypt was involved in many medieval and Renaissance cults, especially in the Rosicrucian and other occult traditions...."[13] Rutherford's judgment placed the *Watch Tower* magazine in the position of explaining, endorsing and selling material on the Pyramid which "was really inspired by Satan for the purpose of misleading the faithful."[14]

---

[12] *New World Translation* (Brooklyn: Watchtower Bible and Tract Society, 1950), p. 793.

[13] Gardner, p. 174.

[14] *Ibid.*, p. 182. For a further treatment on the Great Pyramid, see: Wilbur M. Smith, *Egypt in Biblical Prophecy*, specifically the chapter entitled "The Strange Cult of the Pyramidists," pp. 210-231.

In 1940, The Insitute of Pyramidology was founded by Adam Rutherford in London. Rutherford is the President of the Institute and the Editor of the quarterly, *Pyramidology Magazine.* He also is the author of the five-volume work, *Pyramidology* (four volumes had been published by 1971). Rutherford's works show a familiarity with Russell's ideas.

For those interested, the address of the Institute is: The Institute of Pyramidology, 31 Station Road, Harpenden, Hertforshire, Great Britain.

APPENDIX B

THE FATHERS AND THE WATCHTOWER ON THE 6,000 YEAR TRADITION

The reasoning of the Church Fathers on the six thousand year tradition differs from that of the Watchtower. The Fathers' view was grounded in the six days of creation and the seventh day as a day of rest, the Sabbath. On the basis of II Peter 3:8, the six creative "days" were viewed as 1,000 years in length: "But, beloved, be not ignorant of this one thing, that one day is with the Lord as a thousand years, and a thousand years as one day." Psalm 90:4 was also cited: "For a thousand years in thy sight are but as yesterday . . . ." Therefore, they reasoned, since the six creative "days" were six days of 1,000 years (6,000 years total), six thousand years would be the duration of the world system as it was, followed by a 1,000-year Sabbath rest (Heb. 4).

The Witnesses come to the same result, as far as the 6,000 years of history before God's intervention is concerned, by means of a different line of argument. They reason that the "days" of creation must all be the same in length, as they are all part of one "week." The study of chronology, they state, reveals that the seventh "day" has been going on for almost 6,000 years,[1] and that means there must yet be a 1,000 year reign of Christ. It is then concluded that they

> find the seventh "day" of the creative week to be seven thousand years long. On the basis of the length of the seventh "day" it is therefore reasonable to conclude that each of the other six "days" also was a period of 7,000 years.[2]

---

[1] From 4026 B.C. to 1971 A.D. is just four years short of being 6,000 years.

[2] *The Watchtower*, XCI (February 15, 1970), p. 120.

APPENDIX C

RUSSELL'S CHRONOLOGY AND ITS VERIFICATION

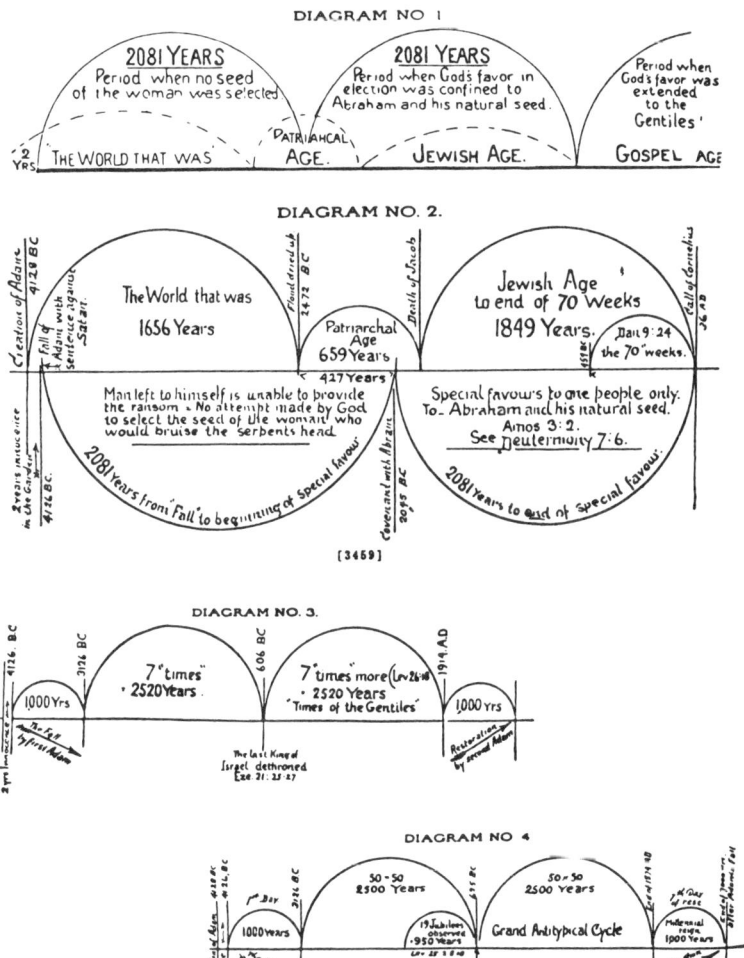

Watch Tower Reprints, IV (November 15, 1904), pp. 3459, 3460.

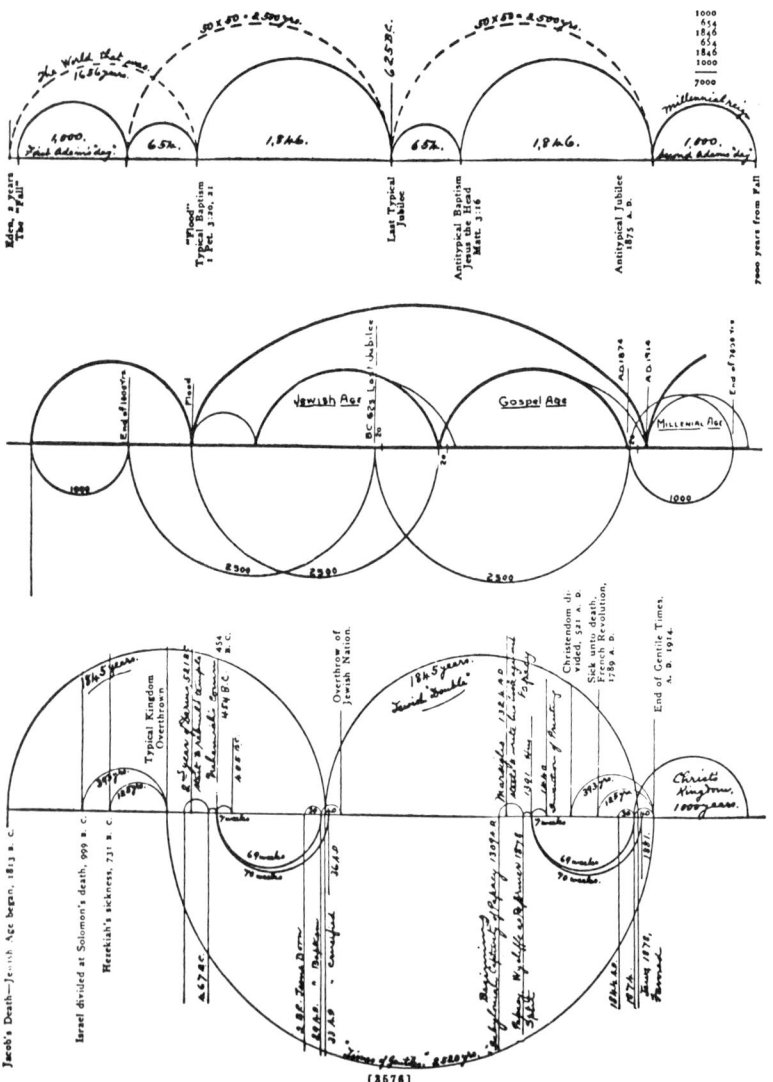

Watch Tower Reprints, IV (June 15, 1905), p. 3576.

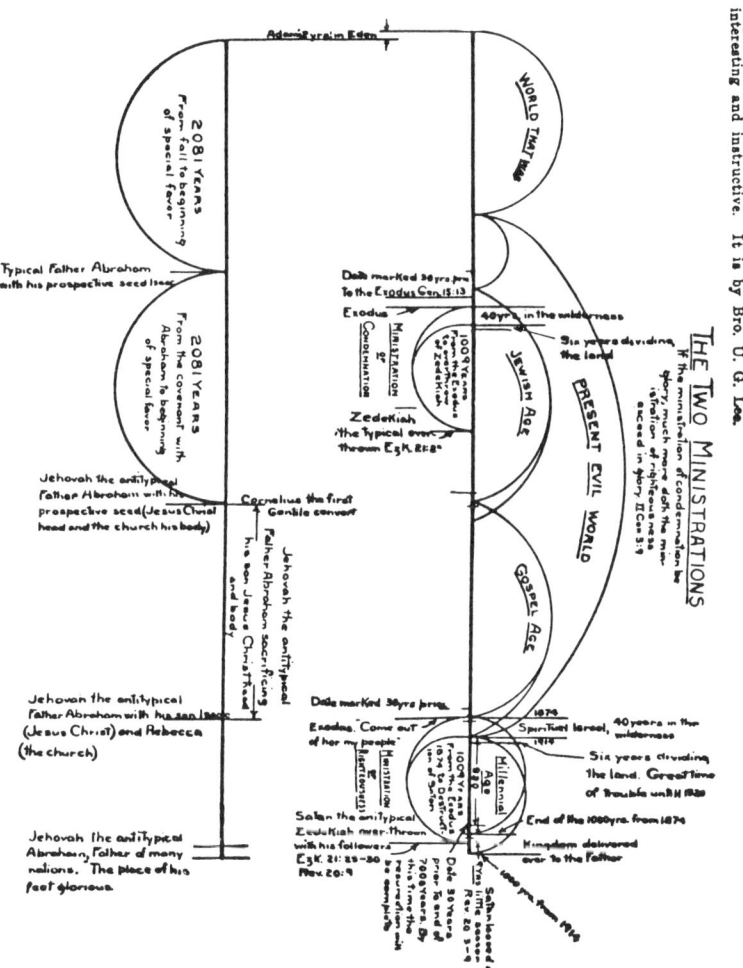

Watch Tower Reprints, IV (June 15, 1905), p. 3579.

APPENDIX D

WHITCOMB AND MORRIS ON ABRIDGED GENEALOGIES

Genesis 11 and the Date of the Flood[1]

GENESIS 11 NEED NOT BE INTERPRETED AS A STRICT CHRONOLOGY

One of the greatest objections to the concept of a geographically universal Deluge in the minds of some scholars today is the fact that there are no historical or archaeological evidences for such a vast catastrophe during the third millennium B.C. (this date being obtained by adding the years of patriarchal maturity given in the Massoretic Text of Genesis 11) or even the fourth millennium B.C. (according to the years given in the Septuagint). Near Eastern cultures apparently have a rather continuous archaeological record (based upon occupation levels and pottery chronology) back to at least the fifth millennium B.C., and it seems impossible to fit a catastrophe of the proportions depicted in Genesis 6-9 into such an archaeological framework. But there are several important reasons for questioning the validity of the strict-chronology interpretation of Genesis 11.

(1) The Number of Years Are Not Totalled

If the list of names and ages in Genesis 11 has been given to us for the purpose of constructing a pre-Abrahamic chronology, it is rather strange that Moses failed to give the *total* number of years from the Flood to Abraham. Of course, it may be objected that he

---

[1] John C. Whitcomb, Jr. and Henry M. Morris, *The Genesis Flood* (Philadelphia: The Presbyterian and Reformed Publishing Company, 1961), pp. 474-483. Reprinted by permission of the publisher.

Genesis 11 and the Date of the Flood

expected the reader to do his own totalling and, therefore, did not add unnecessary words. But Moses took nothing for granted in the reader's ability to add just *two* numbers in the life of each antediluvian patriarch (Gen. 5) in order to ascertain their total life-spans! If the time-span of the *whole* period was one of the important reasons for giving the genealogy, how simple it would have been to give the total, as he did in Exodus 12:40 for the time of Israel's sojourn in Egypt!

(2) The Name and Years of Cainan Do Not Appear in the Hebrew Text

Another reason for questioning Ussher's chronology for Genesis 11 is the evidence that not all the post-diluvian patriarchs are listed in our present Hebrew text. For in Luke's genealogy of Mary, the name "Cainan" appears between "Shelah" and "Arphaxad" (Luke 3:36). The Septuagint translation of Genesis 11 places the name "Cainan" in the same position that Luke does. It is possible, of course, to hold that the name "Cainan" was a later insertion into the Septuagint text and that it did not appear in the original manuscript of Luke. The problem is admittedly a complex one, but for the sake of brevity, we shall simply state our conclusion: the Septuagint *does* give us the full list of *names* as they appeared in the original Hebrew text; but since the *years* for these patriarchs as given in the Septuagint are obviously false, we have no way of determining how old Cainan was at the birth of his first son.[1] Thus, this one omission, even if there are no others, makes it impossible to fix the date of the Flood.

(3) Genesis 5 and 11 Are Perfectly Symmetrical in Form

The fact that Cainan should be included in Genesis 11 has greater implications than might appear at first glance; for the addition of his name puts the genealogies of Genesis 5 and 11 into perfectly sym-

---

[1] C. Robert Fetter ("A Critical Investigation of 'The Second Cainan' in Luke 3:36" Winona Lake, Indiana: Grace Theological Seminary, unpublished critical monograph, 1956), lists the following texts and versions which omit the name of Cainan: (1) all the passages in the Hebrew text (Gen. 10:24; 11:12-13; I Chron. 1:18, 24); (2) the Samaritan Pentateuch; (3) I Chron. 1:24 in the Septuagint; (4) the Targums of Jonathan and Onkelos; (5) the Syriac Version; (6) the Latin Vulgate; and (7) Codex Bezae on Luke 3:36. But those which *do* mention Cainan are: (1) nearly all the Greek manuscripts of Luke 3:36; (2) the Septuagint of Gen. 10:24,

metrical forms. In each case, there are *ten* patriarchs listed, with the *tenth* patriarch having *three* important sons:

1. Adam	1. Shem
2. Seth	2. Arpachshad
3. Enosh	3. Cainan
4. Kenan	4. Shelah
5. Mahalalel	5. Eber
6. Jared	6. Peleg
7. Enoch	7. Reu
8. Methuselah	8. Serug
9. Lamech	9. Nahor
10. Noah	10. Terah
(Shem, Ham, Japheth)	(Abram, Nahor, Haran)

Now this symmetrical arrangement is of great importance in enabling us to determine one important purpose of these genealogies; for a study of the closest parallel to this phenomenon in Scripture, namely, that of the three groups of fourteen names in the first chapter of Matthew, reveals the purposely symmetrical character of such an arrangement of names, possibly as an aid to memorization. If it be objected that in our arrangement of the two lists of patriarchs Shem's name appears twice, it is sufficient to answer that Matthew lists David twice in his arrangement of names too. And even if the name of Cainan were not in the original text, the genealogies of Genesis 5 and 11 would still be symmetrical: Adam to Noah, ten generations; and Shem to Abram, ten generations. These facts may well indicate that it is not necessary to press the numerical data of these chapters into a strict chronology.

(4) *Information Is Given Concerning Each Patriarch Which Is Irrelevant to a Strict Chronology*

Genesis 5:6-8 states that "Seth lived a hundred and five years and begat Enosh: and Seth lived after he begat Enosh eight hundred and

---

11:12-13, and I Chronicles 1:18; (3) the Book of Jubilees; and (4) Demetrius of the 3rd century B.C., according to Polyhistor and Theophilus of Antioch. Apart from the question of Cainan's inclusion in Genesis 11, the Septuagint numbers for the years of the patriarchs at maturity are not trustworthy. The purpose of these translators was apparently not so much to stretch the chronology as it was to make the lives of the patriarchs more symmetrical by having their first born sons after they were 100 years old. "A simple glance at these numbers is sufficient to show that the Hebrew is the original." William Henry Green, "Primeval Chronology," *Bibliotheca Sacra*, XLVII, No. 186 (April, 1890), p. 302.

Genesis 11 and the Date of the Flood

seven years, and begat sons and daughters: and all the days of Seth were nine hundred and twelve years: and he died." Now if the purpose of this genealogy was to provide us with a chronology, all we would need to have is this: "Seth lived a hundred and five years and begat Enosh." But the additional facts which are provided concerning each patriarch indicate that the purpose of these genealogies was more than simply chronological. Their major purpose was to show us how faithfully God guarded the Messianic line (Gen. 3:15; 9:26) even in ages of universal apostasy (Gen. 6:1-12; 11:1-9); to impress upon us "the vigor and grandeur of humanity in those old days of the world's prime";[1] to demonstrate the fulfillment of the curse of Genesis 2:17 by the melancholy repetition of the phrase "and he died"; to show by the shorter life spans of postdiluvian patriarchs and by the omission of their total years of life the tightening grip of the Edenic curse upon the human body; and to make "the record end in terms of the command of 9:1, which was so vitally important in view of the Flood," by omitting the words "and he died" in the genealogy of Genesis 11.[2] Since, therefore, so many pedagogical purposes are evident in these two genealogies that have nothing to do with the actual length of the overall period, it is unnecessary to press them into a rigid chronological system.

(5) *The Postdiluvian Patriarchs Could Not Have Been Contemporaries of Abram*

If the strict-chronology interpretation of Genesis 11 is correct, *all* the postdiluvian patriarchs, including Noah, would still have been living when Abram was fifty years old; *three* of those who were born before the earth was divided (Shem, Shelah, and Eber) would have actually outlived Abram; and *Eber,* the father of Peleg, not only would have outlived Abram, but would have lived for two years after Jacob arrived in Mesopotamia to work for Laban!

On the face of it, such a situation would seem astonishing, if not almost incredible. And the case is further strengthened by the clear and twice-repeated statement of Joshua that Abram's "fathers," including Terah, were idolaters when they dwelt "of old time beyond

---

[1] Benjamin B. Warfield, *Biblical and Theological Studies,* edited by Samuel G. Craig (Philadelphia: The Presbyterian & Reformed Publishing Co., 1952), p. 244.
[2] Oswald T. Allis, *The Five Books of Moses* (Philadelphia: The Presbyterian & Reformed Pub. Co., 1943), p. 263.

the River" (Joshua 24:2, 14, 15). If all the postdiluvian patriarchs, including Noah and Shem, were still living in Abram's day, this statement implies that they had all fallen into idolatry by then. This conclusion is surely wrong, and therefore the premise on which it is based must be wrong. Consequently, it seems that the strict-chronology view must be set aside in order to allow for the death of these patriarchs long before the time of Abram.

(6) *The Bible Implies a Great Antiquity For the Tower of Babel*

If we accept 2167 B.C. as the year of Abram's birth,[1] the Flood must have occurred in the year 2459 B.C. and the judgment of the Tower of Babel between 2358 and 2119 B.C. (the lifetime of Peleg) according to the strict-chronology interpretation.

When we turn to the Genesis account of Abram's journeys, however, we discover the international scene to have been quite different from that suggested by the above-mentioned dates for the Flood and the judgment of Babel. Abram is certainly not depicted as one of the early pioneers from the land of Shinar who migrated to western territories that were only beginning to be settled 200 years after the judgment of Babel. Quite to the contrary, the Bible implies that the world of Abram's day, with its civilizations and cities, was ancient already; and we are left with the unmistakable impression that its peoples had long since been divided "after their families, after their tongues, in their lands, in their nations" (Gen. 10:5, 20, 31).

As we follow Abram in his wanderings, from Ur of the Chaldees to the land of Canaan, filled to overflowing with "the Kenite, and the Kenizzite, the Amorite, and the Canaanite, and the Girgashite, and the Jebusite" (Gen. 15:19-21); and then follow him down into the land of Egypt with its Pharoah and its princes (12:15); and then see him going to Lot's rescue in the vicinity of Damascus after Lot and other captives from the five Cities of the Plain had been deported by the kings of Shinar, Ellaser, Elam, and Goiim (14:1-

---

[1] According to Edwin R. Thiele (*The Mysterious Numbers of the Hebrew Kings* [Chicago: University of Chicago Press, 1951]), 931 B.C. was the date of the division of the kingdom at the death of Solomon. Following I Kings 6:1 and Exodus 12:40, we arrive at 1877 B.C. for the entrance of Jacob into Egypt. Since Jacob was 130 years old at this time (Gen. 47:9), he was born in 2007 B.C. Isaac was 60 when Jacob was born (Gen. 25:26), and Abraham was 100 when Isaac was born (Gen. 21:5). Therefore, Abraham was born in 2167 B.C.

16); and then see him being met by a priest-king of Salem (14:18); and later see him coming into contact with a Philistine king (20:2) and Hittite landowners (23:2-20), we cannot help but feel that the judgment of God upon the Tower of Babel must have occurred many centuries before the time of Abram.[1]

This impression is confirmed by Jeremiah (47:4) and Amos (9:7), who inform us that the Philistines came into Canaan, not from Shinar but rather from the west from Caphtor, which is the island of Crete. And Moses tells us that before the Philistines ever came to Canaan from Caphtor, the southwestern section of Canaan had been occupied by the Avvim (Deut. 2:23). Thus, the Bible implies that Babel was judged long before 2358 B.C.

(7) The Messianic Links Were Seldom Firstborn Sons

Within the genealogy of Genesis 11 there are additional indications that we are dealing with something other than a chronology. One of these is found in the statement of Genesis 11:26—"And Terah lived seventy years, and begat Abram, Nahor, and Terah." Taking this statement at face value, one might well conclude that Terah became the father of triplets in his seventieth year (even as his grandson Isaac became the father of twins in his sixtieth year), Abram being the firstborn of the triplets. We are somewhat astonished, however, to discover upon further investigation that Abram was *not* the firstborn of the three and that Terah was *not* seventy, but rather one hundred and thirty years old when Abram was born!

In Genesis 11:32 we read that "the days of Terah were two hundred and five years: and Terah died in Haran"; while in 12:4 we find that "Abram was seventy and five years old when he departed out of Haran." Thus, if Abram left Haran to go to Canaan after Terah's death, Abram must have been born when his father was 130 years old. The possibility of Abram's leaving Terah in Haran sixty years before Terah finally died is excluded by Stephen's statement that "from thence, when his father was dead, God removed him into

---

[1] Byron C. Nelson, *Before Abraham* (Minneapolis: Augsburg Pub. House, 1948), p. 100, points out that Genesis mentions 26 cities in Canaan alone during the days of Abraham. Seven of these are said to have had kings. Presumably the five cities of the Plain, at least, had been in existence there so long that their cup of iniquity was already full to overflowing (cf. Gen. 15:16).

The Genesis Flood

this land, wherein ye now dwell" (Acts 7:4).[1] In the light of these considerations, we may paraphrase Genesis 11:26 as follows: "And Terah lived seventy years and begat the first of his three sons, the most important of whom (not because of age but because of the Messianic line) was Abram."

It is quite possible that only a small number of the patriarchs listed in Genesis 11 were firstborn sons. A comparison of 11:10 with 5:32 and 8:13 suggests that Shem was not. A comparison of 11:10 with 10:22 suggests that Arpachshad was not. And we have already seen that Abram was not. Actually, *not one* of the Messianic ancestors in Genesis, whose family background is known in any detail, such as Abel, Seth, Abram, Isaac, Jacob, Judah, and Perez, was a firstborn son. The year of begetting a first son, known in the Old Testament as "the beginning of strength," was an important year in the life of the Israelite (Gen. 49:3, Deut. 21:17, Psa. 78:51, and Psa. 105:36). It is this year, then, and not necessarily the year of the birth of the Messianic link, that is given in each case in Genesis 11. Thus we have clear evidence for the possible addition of a limited number of years from the lives of some of these patriarchs to the total of years from the Flood to Abraham.[2]

---

[1] F. F. Bruce, in his *Commentary on the Book of Acts* (Grand Rapids: Wm. B. Eerdmans Pub. Co., 1955), pp. 146-147, attempts to sidestep the problem by adopting the view that Stephen was using a Greek text of Genesis 11:32 that gave Terah's age at death at 145 (like the Samaritan Pentateuch). The serious implications of such a view may be seen in the more recent statement of Everett F. Harrison, "The Phenomena of Scripture," in *Revelation and the Bible,* edited by Carl F. H. Henry (Grand Rapids: Baker Book House, 1958), p. 249: "Does inspiration require that a Biblical writer should be preserved from error in the use of sources? Presumably when Stephen asserted that Abraham left Haran for Canaan after his father's death (Acts 7:4), he was following a type of Septuagintal text such as Philo used, for the latter has the same statement (*Migration of Abraham,* 177). The Hebrew text of Genesis will not permit this, since the figures given in Genesis 11:26, 32 and 12:4 demand that Terah continued to live for 60 years after Abraham left Haran." The principal objection to the interpretation we have advocated is that Abraham would not have staggered at the thought of a 100-year-old man begetting a son if his own father was 130 when he was born (Gen. 17:17, Rom. 4:19). But it should also be remembered that Abraham did not think it impossible to beget a child by Hagar when he was 86 (Gen. 16:16) or to beget children by Keturah when he was over 140 (Gen. 25:1, cf. 23:1, 25:20). Even as Isaac experienced a serious failing in health 43 years before he died (27:1), so also Abraham may have failed in health by the time he was 99. In response to his renewed faith in God and in God's promise (Rom. 4:19), his body, which was "now as good as dead," must have been renewed by God to live out the remaining 75 years and to beget many more children (Gen. 25:1-7). Thus, the emphasis of Genesis 17:17 may well be the physical condition of Abraham and Sarah at this particular period in their lives, and not so much their actual age. R. C. H. Lenski, in *The Interpretation of the Acts of the Apostles* (Columbus:

Genesis 11 and the Date of the Flood

(8) *The Term "Begat" Sometimes Refers to Ancestral Relationships*

Such terms as "begat" and "the son of," which in English imply a father-son relationship, sometimes have a much wider connotation in the Bible. In Matthew 1:8, we read that "Joram *begat* Uzziah," but three generations are omitted. In I Chronicles 26:24, we are told that "Shebuel the son of Gershom, the son of Moses, was ruler over the treasures" in the days of David. Here we have 400 years of generations skipped over between Shebuel and Gershom. But the most interesting case of all, in our opinion, is to be found in Exodus 6:20. Here we read that "Amram took him Jochebed his father's sister to wife; and she bare him Aaron and Moses: and the years of the life of Amram were a hundred and thirty and seven years." Now anyone reading this statement as it stands by itself would be forced to conclude that Aaron and Moses were the actual sons of Amram and Jochebed; for the text clearly states that "she bare him Aaron and Moses," and immediately following this we are given the number of the years that Amram lived, in a manner strikingly similar to that of the genealogy of Genesis 5. So it is with profound amazement that we turn to Numbers 3:17-19, 27-28, and discover that in the days of Moses, "the family of the *Amramites*," together with the families of Amram's three brothers (Izhar, Hebron, and Uzziel), numbered 8,600! Unless we are willing to grant that the first cousins of Moses and Aaron had over 8,500 living male offspring, we must admit that Amram was an *ancestor* of Moses and Aaron, separated from them by a span of 300 years! In the light of this, it is significant that the

---

Lutheran Book Concern, 1934), p. 259, concludes his discussion of the problem as follows: "Aside from the inspiration by which Stephen spoke and Luke wrote, it does seem that in the simple matter of adding a few figures, Stephen (Philo too) would not have made such palpable errors. The real motive lying behind these claims that discrepancies exist in the account is the denial of the inspiration and inerrancy of the Scriptures."

[2] John Urquhart, *How Old Is Man?* (London: James Nisbet & Co., 1904), pp. 101ff., suggested that since Abram was born near the half-way mark of the period between the birth of Terah's first son and the time of Terah's death, the same situation might have been true, on the average, for the other postdiluvian patriarchs as well. By averaging the two extreme possibilities, he arrived at 1668 years as the probable interval between the Flood and the birth of Abram. If, as we pointed out above (note 1, page 478), Abram was born in 2167 B.C., this would date the Flood at 3835 B.C. But Urquhart did not take into consideration the possible ancestral usage of the term "begat."

The Genesis Flood

names of the actual parents of Moses and Aaron are not recorded in the narrative of Exodus 2:1-10.[1]

Keeping in mind this remarkable and enlightening example of how the Jews compiled their genealogies, we turn our attention once again to Genesis 11. Taking as a case for special study the central section of that genealogy, we read in verses 16-19:

> And Eber lived four and thirty years, and begat Peleg; and Eber lived after he begat Peleg four hundred and thirty years, and begat sons and daughters. And Peleg lived thirty years, and begat Reu: and Peleg lived after he begat Reu two hundred and nine years, and begat sons and daughters.

For at least two reasons, this section of the postdiluvian patriarchal genealogy is unusual and calls for careful consideration. First, we find here a sudden drop in the life-span of the patriarchs that is unparalleled in the entire genealogy. Until the time of Eber, no postdiluvian patriarch is said to have lived less than 433 years. But now, without any explanation, the life-span drops to 239 years and never exceeds that number again! This represents a permanent drop in life-span of 45%, as opposed to the 23% drop from Shem to Eber.

The second peculiarity about this section is that it contains the name of Peleg, of whom it is said (in 10:25) that "in his days was the earth divided." It has been generally conceded by Old Testament scholars that this explanation has reference to the judgment of Babel, at which time "Jehovah scattered them abroad from thence upon the face of all the earth" (11:8, cf. 10:25). But it is difficult to understand why it should be said only of *Peleg*, that "in his days was the earth divided," if, on the assumption that Genesis 11 is a strict chronology, Noah, Shem, Arpachshad, Shelah, and Eber (and probably Cainan) were still living throughout the entire lifetime of Peleg.

All of this leads us to submit the following proposition: at least in *this* section of Genesis 11, if not in other sections, we have warrant for assuming that the term "begat" is to be understood in the ancestral sense. From the fact that there is a sudden and permanent drop in the life-span between Eber and Peleg and also from the fact

---

[1] See John D. Davis, *A Dictionary of the Bible* (4th ed., rev.; Philadelphia: The Westminster Press, 1929), p. 195.

Genesis 11 and the Date of the Flood

that Peleg is the only patriarch who is recorded as having lived at the time of the judgment upon Babel, we feel justified in assuming that Peleg was a distant *descendant* of Eber.

Now the objection might be raised at this point that Genesis 10:25 cannot allow for such a view; for in that passage we read that "unto Eber were born two sons: the name of the one was Peleg; for in his days was the earth divided; and his brother's name was Joktan." How, then, could Peleg be a distant descendant of Eber, if we are told in this passage that Eber had two sons of whom one was Peleg? Would not such a statement preclude the possibility of a merely ancestral relationship?

Indeed, this would be a serious objection, were it not for our parallel case in Exodus 6:20. There we found that *two sons were born unto Amram*. But from the third chapter of Numbers we also discovered that Moses and Aaron were only two of 8,600 living descendants of Amram's father. Now the very same thing could be true of Genesis 10:25, where we read that *two sons were born unto Eber*. By analogy with Exodus 6:20, then, it seems quite possible that Peleg and Joktan were only two of the many living descendants of Eber at the time of God's judgment upon Babel.

In summarizing the arguments of this entire discussion, we may say that the lack of an overall total of years for the period from the Flood to Abraham, the absence of Cainan's name and years in the Hebrew text, the symmetrical form of the genealogies of Genesis 5 and 11, the inclusion of data that are irrelevant to a strict chronology, the impossibility of all the postdiluvian patriarchs being contemporaries of Abraham, the Biblical indications of a great antiquity for the judgment of Babel, the fact that the Messianic links were seldom firstborn sons, and the analogy of "begat" being used in the ancestral sense allow the existence of gaps of an undetermined length in the patriarchal genealogy of Genesis 11.

APPENDIX E

ARE THE GENESIS DAYS 7,000 YEARS LONG?

While it must be acknowledged that there are many variant ideas concerning the meaning of the word "day" (Hebrew, *yom*) in the Genesis account of creation, there is, as Dr. Raymond Surburg states, "An impressive amount of evidence favoring the view that the 'days' referred to in connection with the creative activity of God were not long periods but solar days of approximately 24 hours." [1] What is the evidence?

1. It is a basic principle in Biblical interpretation that words should be understood in their basic and literal meaning "unless there are compelling reasons for adopting a figurative or derived interpretation. Such reasons are absent from Gen. 1." [2] The authors of *The Genesis Flood* state:" . . .Since there apparently is no contextual basis for understanding these days in any sort of symbolic sense, it is an act of both faith and reason to accept them, literally, as real days." [3]

2. "The Hebrew dictionaries of Buhl, Brown, Briggs, Driver, and Koenig do not record the interpretation of *yom* in the Hexaemeron [the six days of the creation] as a long period of time." [4] The March 1953 issue of the *Journal of the American Scientific Affiliation* included "A Brief Note on the Translation of the Word 'Day' in Genesis 1." The author of the article had written nine different professors of Oriental languages at nine universities in England, America and Canada. He asked how "the Hebrew word *"yom"* (day) as used in Genesis 1 accompanied

---

[1] Raymond Surburg, "In the Beginning God Created," Chapter 2 of *Darwin, Evolution and Creation* (St. Louis: Concordia Publishing House, 1959), p. 59.

[2] *Ibid.*

[3] John C. Whitcomb, Jr. and Henry M. Morris, *The Genesis Flood* (Philadelphia: Presbyterian and Reformed Publishing Company, 1961), p. 228.

[4] Surburg, pp. 59, 60.

by a numeral should be properly translated: (a) a day, as commonly understood (b) an age (c) either an age or a day without preference." The "seven who replied gave the answer in each instance as 'a day, as commonly understood.' One of those who replied, Prof. Robert H. Pfeiffer of Harvard University, added the word 'of 24 hours' to his answer."[5] Marcus Dods stated: "If the word 'day' in these chapters does not mean a period of 24 hours, the interpretation of Scripture is hopeless."[6] Numerous similar quotations could be cited.

3. "When in the Old Testament *yom* is associated with a definite numeral, solar days are meant. (Gen 7:11; 8:14; 17:12; Ex. 12:6, and numerous other passages)"[7]

In the Genesis account of creation, as Dr. Henry Morris states, not only is the noun (day) modified by a numerical adjective ("first day," "second day," etc.), but

> the boundaries of the time period in each case [are indicated] as "evening and morning." Either one of these devices would suffice to limit the meaning of *yom* to that of a solar day, and when both are used, there could be no better or surer way possible for the writer to convey the intended meaning of a literal solar day![8]

The word "day" is also clearly defined the first time it is used in the Bible, in Genesis 1:5: "And God called the light Day, and the darkness he called Night. And the evening and the morning were the first day." Genesis 1:14-19, in reference to the fourth creative day further clarifies the meaning of "day" and "days."

> ... Let there be lights in the firmament of the heaven to divide the day from the night; and let them be for signs, and for seasons, and for days, and years: ... the greater light to rule the day, and the lesser light to rule the night .... And the evening and the morning were the fourth day.

4. "The wording of the Genesis account seems to indicate a short time for the creative acts described.... Instantaneous action seems to be what the writer stresses." This is illustrated by Genesis 1:11, 12. God commanded: "Earth, sprout sprouts!" Verse 12 records the immediate response to the command: "The

---

[5] P. 15.

[6] Surburg, p. 60.

[7] *Ibid.*

[8] Henry M. Morris, "The Day-Age Theory," *Creation Research Society Quarterly*, June, 1971, p. 73.

earth caused the plants to go out."[9]

5. "The interpretation of *yom* as a solar day is the interpretation which other portions of Scripture indicate."[10] This is evident in Exodus 20:8-11 when the Sabbath is instituted.

> Remember the sabbath *day*, to keep it holy. Six *days* shalt thou labor, and do all thy work: But the seventh *day* is the sabbath of the Lord thy God . . . . For in six *days* the Lord made heaven and earth, the sea, and all that in them is, and rested the seventh *day:* wherefore the Lord blessed the sabbath *day*, and hallowed it.

As the words clearly indicate, the six days of God's creation are identical in length with the six days of man's work week. The strength of the analogy would lose its force if the creative days were not solar days.

6. There is no doubt that the word "day" can be used to express different meanings, as any Bible dictionary indicates. But as a Witness publication correctly states: "The Bible context indicates the sense in which the word 'day' applies."[11] The context of Genesis 1, as already stated, does not require changing the normal meaning of the word. When the Witnesses cite Genesis 2:4 (*"in the day* that the Lord God made the earth and the heavens"), it is proper to see the word "day" used here in other than a literal sense. Numbers 7:1-84 presents an interesting parallel to Genesis 1 and 2 in the use of the word "day" as a literal day (verses 12-83) and as the word is used comprehensively (verse 84). "In both instances we have first a record of details which occurred in 'days' of 24 hours' duration, and then we have the word used *comprehensively* of what has been previously set forth in detail."[12] Genesis 2:4 offers no support for giving the days of Genesis 1 other than a literal meaning.

7. The Witnesses' view that the Genesis days are 7,000 years in length has already been exploded by what has been demonstrated elsewhere in this book — the fact that far more

---

[9] Surburg, p. 60.

[10] *Ibid.*, pp. 60, 61.

[11] *All Scripture Is Inspired of God and Beneficial* (Brooklyn: Watchtower Bible and Tract Society, 1963), p. 278.

[12] Arthur F. Williams, "The Genesis Account of Creation," *Creation Research Society Annual*, May, 1965, p. 10.

than 6,000 years have transpired since Adam's creation (with the last 1,000 years taken up by the Kingdom reign of Christ). Since this is the case, the Witnesses' understanding of Genesis 2:2,3 and Hebrews 4:1-10 is incorrect. Their use of such passages as Psalm 90:4 and I Peter 3:8 in the interpretation of the days of Genesis is not only poor exegesis, but poor theology as well.[13]

---

[13] For further discussion of these passages and some of the other objections to the 24-hour day view of the creative days see: Morris, pp. 72-75; Surburg, pp. 57f.; Louis Berkhof, *Systematic Theology* (Grand Rapids: Wm. B. Eerdmans Publishing Company, 1938), pp. 138f.; Williams, pp. 7-13.

Easy Street
Easy Street
Easy Street
Easy Street
Easy Street
Easy Street
Easy Street
Easy Street
Easy Street
Easy Street
Easy Street